# A 12 Week Bible Study from the Devotional Book "Beyond the Sunday Sermon"

RONALD W. HOLMES, PH.D.

authorHOUSE

AuthorHouse™
1663 Liberty Drive
Bloomington, IN 47403
www.authorhouse.com
Phone: 833-262-8899

© 2024 Ronald W. Holmes, Ph.D. All rights reserved.

No part of this book may be reproduced, stored in a retrieval system, or transmitted by any means without the written permission of the author.

Published by AuthorHouse  02/27/2024

ISBN: 979-8-8230-2105-0 (sc)
ISBN: 979-8-8230-2106-7 (hc)
ISBN: 979-8-8230-2107-4 (e)

Library of Congress Control Number: 2024901513

Print information available on the last page.

Any people depicted in stock imagery provided by Getty Images are models, and such images are being used for illustrative purposes only.
Certain stock imagery © Getty Images.

This book is printed on acid-free paper.

Because of the dynamic nature of the Internet, any web addresses or links contained in this book may have changed since publication and may no longer be valid. The views expressed in this work are solely those of the author and do not necessarily reflect the views of the publisher, and the publisher hereby disclaims any responsibility for them.

# CONTENTS

Acknowledgement ..................................................................... vii
Dedication ................................................................................. ix
Introduction .............................................................................. xi

## Bible Study Messages, Outline of Services & Visual Slides

Week 1 –  Living Beyond Blindness: I Need to See ..................... 1
            Outline of Service ............................................................ 6
            Visual Slides .................................................................... 7

Week 2 –  Singing The Lord's Song in A Strange Land ............ 11
            Outline of Service .......................................................... 16
            Visual Slides .................................................................. 18

Week 3 –  Never Say Die ........................................................... 22
            Outline of Service .......................................................... 27
            Visual Slides .................................................................. 29

Week 4 –  The Gift of Prayer ..................................................... 33
            Outline of Service .......................................................... 39
            Visual Slides .................................................................. 41

Week 5 –  Believe the Promise .................................................. 45
            Outline of Service .......................................................... 51
            Visual Slides .................................................................. 53

Week 6 –   Go Thy Way! Give God Thanks!............................................... 57
              Outline of Service................................................................. 64
              Visual Slides......................................................................... 66

Week 7 –   Be Great! Serve! ................................................................... 71
              Outline of Service................................................................. 78
              Visual Slides......................................................................... 80

Week 8 –   The Gift of Jesus .................................................................. 85
              Outline of Service................................................................. 93
              Visual Slides......................................................................... 95

Week 9 –   The Promise of the Passover............................................... 100
              Outline of Service............................................................... 107
              Visual Slides....................................................................... 109

Week 10 – The Power of Living on "Yet" .................................................. 114
              Outline of Service............................................................... 122
              Visual Slides....................................................................... 124

Week 11 – Trust in God ............................................................................ 129
              Outline of Service............................................................... 136
              Visual Slides....................................................................... 138

Week 12 – Remember, Repent, Return & Respect............................ 142
              Outline of Service............................................................... 150
              Visual Slides....................................................................... 152

References ................................................................................................ 157
Author's Background ............................................................................... 159
Other Books Of The Holmes Education Post, LLC ............................... 161

# ACKNOWLEDGEMENT

I am grateful for Reverend Frederick Douglas Newbill, Sr. pastor of First Timothy Baptist Church in Jacksonville, Florida for allowing me to use my new book titled *"Beyond the Sunday Sermon: A 52 Devotional from the teaching and preaching of Reverend Dr. R.B. Holmes Jr,"* as a resource to facilitate bible study at the church in person and online.

I would like to thank all the church members, family members, and friends of First Timothy who attended and participated in the bible study. I particularly appreciate all the church members who contributed their time and energy to the journal discussions during the 12 weeks of bible study.

Without reservation, I would also like to thank my wife, Constance Holmes for being the editor for the book, creating the PowerPoint slides, developing the outline of the services, and organizing the journal discussion component of the bible study.

# DEDICATION

In this world, we will experience trials, tribulations, hardships, and disappointments. This bible study book provides examples of people in the bible who have had similar tribulations to the experiences we are facing today.

It is my hope that this book will bring readers closer to God by relying on him to help them overcome their hardships just as he has done for many people in the bible.

I proudly dedicate this book to my grandparents, Clem and Louise Johnson. As a child in the 1960s, I gained real-world business experience from them while working in their grocery store in Americus, Georgia. They taught me to politely greet every customer who entered the store with the question, "Something for you?" In modern day vernacular, the question would be, "May I help you?"

Also, I gratefully dedicate this book to my parents, R.B. and Lucille Holmes. They have been the backbone to my achievement and accolades in all endeavors. They constantly taught me the value of prayer, life, family, school, and work. Through the years, I learned so many lessons from them. Specifically, my father taught me about perseverance and credibility as he worked long hours and assisted his friends and three sons in getting good jobs with his employer. My mother taught me about fortitude as she set the example by going back to school and earning a college degree and teaching high school for over twenty-two years after raising eight children. Her perservance showed me the value of educaton and taught me that it is never too late to pursue your dream. Her motivation influenced all of us to attend college and earn a bachelor's degree.

I prayerfully dedicate this book to my grandparents and parents. I have achieved a life-time dream and an appreciation for life through their prayers, guidance, mentoring, coaching, teaching, and giving to people.

# INTRODUCTION

In 2023, my minister Reverend Frederick Newbill Sr., wanted to relaunch and revive our Wednesday night bible study at First Timothy Baptist Church from a three-year lap due to the pandemic. He raised the critical question to the church: "What would make the members commit to attending every week for Wednesday night bible study? "I suggested that we utilize the devotional book, *"Beyond the Sunday Sermon"* as our text. The plan was to have various bodies of the church (ministers, deacons, and Sunday school teachers) to be responsible for delivery. My pastor asked me to take on the facilitator role. Respectfully, I said yes; and I prayerfully designed a program that would include various design elements.

As a former teacher and administrator coupled with an understating of adult learning theory, this bible study was designed to include PowerPoint slides, gospel songs, and scenes from popular movies to contextualize the learning. This book, *"A 12 Week Bible Study from the Devotional Book "Beyond the Sunday Sermon,"* shares the messages that were created using the theme, "Just Say Yes!" The book also provides an outline of each bible study in a 60-minute format so key participants of the church (ministers, facilitators, and technology support staff) can easily understand their roles and follow the services as planned.

We hope that these 12 messages will encourage other churches and groups to continue their journey to learn and live the word of God, as well as expand how they use the book, *"Beyond the Sunday Sermon."*

# BIBLE STUDY MESSAGES, OUTLINE OF SERVICES & VISUAL SLIDES

WEEK 1

# Living Beyond Blindness: I Need to See

There is an old saying that you can't see the forest for the trees. If that is the case, I advise you to live beyond blindness, get rid of those trees or anything that is blocking you to see. If necessary, be like the man who climbed the sycamore tree to see Jesus. Or be like the woman who touched the hem of Jesus' garment so she could be healed.

Good evening members and friends of First Timothy Baptist Church. I would like to thank Reverend Newbill for allowing me to play a role in relaunching the Wednesday Night Bible Service; and using the book titled "Beyond the Sunday Sermon." I had a different teaching process in mind for the bible service, but in the spiritual context of the song by Brian Wilson, I just said yes to Reverend Newbill that I will follow his lead to facilitate the service.

The teaching style for this bible service will be in the format of writing an essay that includes the introduction, body, and conclusion. Thus, we will (1) read an excerpt of the Sunday Sermon and Scripture; (2) discuss the three key points from the Sunday Sermon lesson; (3) provide concrete details to support the key points; and (4) summarize the lesson with scriptures and questions from the daily Journal.

At this time, Constance Holmes my wife of 32 years and editor of my 26 books from The Holmes Education Post, will come and read the excerpt of the lesson and scripture. Afterwards, I will highlight the three key points for the lesson on Living Beyond Blindness: I Need to See!

Thank you, Constance, for eloquently reading the excerpts of the lesson and scripture. You are the apple of my eye. Now, let's look at the three key points for the lesson (1) faith believes even when you can't see; (2) faith believes regardless of the opposition; and (3) faith believes in the impossible.

## Key Point 1

Faith believes even when you can't see. Faith is the substance of things hoped for, the evidence of things not seen (Hebrews 11:1). Just like blind Bartimaeus, we must demonstrate our faith in the Lord. We must recognize the goodness and blessings of the Lord, faithfully ask Jesus to have mercy on us, and tell him what we want (Mark 10: 46-47). In fact, Mark 11: 24 reminds us that "what things soever ye desire, when ye pray, believe that ye receive them, and ye shall have them."

On this note, I am reminded of an amazing story I witnessed several months ago of a man who collapsed in a swimming pool, lost his sight, and needed a blessing from the Lord. As the man was collapsing in the swimming pool, the man asked his wife, "Do you see Ronald?" The wife yelled spontaneously Ronald! When I heard my name called, I got out of the swimming pool and ran quickly to the area of the pool where the man collapsed; and I helped the lifeguards get the man out of the water. I even gave some instructions unconsciously such as grab his legs and arms so we could get the man's entire body out of the water. To give the man some space, I moved about four feet away from him and the lifeguard. As a lifeguard was giving CPR to him, the lifeguard suddenly screamed, he stopped breathing! I dropped immediately to my knees and prayed for the man's life. The man stopped breathing and could not see, but faith believes even when you can't see. As I stood from praying, simultaneously, the lifeguard shouted, he started back breathing; and I immediately dropped to my knees again and thanked the Lord for restoring the man's life. A week later the man found my telephone number and called me from the hospital. In his own words, the man thanked me for "taking care of business and telling everybody what to do" when his body failed him, and he could not breathe nor see. This story was not about me. Normally, I would be finished with swimming but this day I decided to swim a little longer; so when the man said to his wife, "Do you see Ronald," I was right where I was supposed to be. I believe (First Timothy) this story was about the power of prayer, the goodness and blessing of the Lord, and how the Lord can direct your path and put you somewhere for a particular reason; and I believe this story was about a testament of the amazing grace of the Lord who saved a man that was blind but now can see. Do I have a witness that faith believes even when you can't see?

## Key Point 2:

Secondly, faith believes regardless of the opposition. James Cleveland raised the question in the song titled, "Where is your faith in God" during sickness, trouble, unemployment, brokenness, and addiction to bad habits. First Timothy, where is your faith in God when people try to get you to stay home instead of going to church? Where is your faith in God when people try to stop you from worshiping the Lord? Just like blind Bartimaeus who refused to be persuaded by the people in Jericho and adamantly asked Jesus to have mercy on him (Mark 10:48), go get your blessing. Just like the man who climbed the sycamore tree to see Jesus, go get your blessing. Just like the woman who touched the hem of Jesus' garment to be healed, go get your blessing. Just like the man who wrestled with the Lord all night long until he blessed him, go get your blessing; and just like the song written by Mary Mary, go get it, go get it, go get your blessing. It's your time! Go get your blessing. Keep the faith and ask Jesus to have mercy on you regardless of the opposition.

## Key Point 3:

Thirdly, faith believes in the impossible. With God, nothing is impossible. Jesus made blind Bartimaeus' enemies his footstool. He told them to bring Bartimaeus to him. In preparation to see Jesus, Bartimaeus took off his garment. Jesus asked him what do you want? Bartimaeus said, "Lord that I might receive my sight." Because of Bartimaeus' faith, Jesus granted his request to see and Bartimaeus followed him (Mark 49-52). Just like Bartimaeus, we must demonstrate our faith in the Lord, get rid of our baggage, follow Jesus, and allow him to do the impossible in our lives. We must allow Jesus to do what no man could do when we are faced with trials and tribulations in our lives as illustrated in the song by Pastor Mike Jr. Take a Listen to the song.

In summary, faith believes even when you can't see; faith believes regardless of the opposition; and faith believes in the impossible. As time permits, let's reflect on some of the daily Journal questions from the book such as What is the Power of Prayer? How do you walk by faith and not by sight? and How has the Lord been the "bread of life" in your household for believing in him? Constance will lead the discussion by first reading the scripture for a question and then providing her personal reflection to the question. She will be followed by others who would like to share their reflections to the questions as well.

We are now at the end of the bible service. I hope you have gained something from this service. I look forward to your participation in next Wednesday's lesson titled, Singing the Lord's Song in a Strange Land (Pages 202 – 206). The scripture is Psalm 137: 1-4. Please feel free to invite a guest to join us at the church or online; and spread the word about the service through social media platforms such as Facebook, Tik Tok, Twitter, Instagram, and LinkedIn. If anyone needs a book, you can purchase it online from Amazon.com, Barnes & Noble or AuthorHouse. You can also go to the website of The Holmes Education Post and read some articles about the book.

Now, we will have closing remarks from our pastor, Reverend Newbill.

Ronald W. Holmes, Ph.D.

# Week 1: Outline of Service

Outline of Service<br>
First Timothy Baptist Church<br>
Wednesday Night Bible Service<br>
7:00PM – 8:00PM<br>
September 6, 2023

Message: Living Beyond Blindness: I Need To See
   from the book "Beyond the Sunday Sermon" (Pages 197 - 201)

Scripture: St. Mark 10:46 – 52 KJV

| Time | What | By Whom | Music to play or Visual to Display |
|---|---|---|---|
| 6:55PM – 7:00PM | Music: I'll Say Yes by Brian Courtney Wilson | Media Ministry to play song | Play music video/song – I'll Say Yes |
| 7:00PM -7:05PM | Prayer and Intro of Wednesday Night Bible Service | Reverend Frederick Newbill | Show Slide 1 – Welcome to Wednesday Night Bible Service |
| 7:05PM – 7:10PM | Greetings & Teaching Method | Dr. Ronald Holmes | Show Slide 1 – Welcome to Wednesday Night Bible Service |
| 7:10PM – 7:15PM | Reading the Excerpt of Sunday Sermon & Scripture | Constance Holmes | Slide 2 – Living Beyond Blindness: I Want to See |
| 7:15PM – 7:35PM | • Three Key Points from the Message<br>• Supporting Details from the Message | Dr. Ronald Holmes | Slide 3-6 – Key Messages |
| 7:35PM –7:40PM | • Song:<br>• Impossible – Pastor Mike Jr. | Media Ministry to play song | Play music video/song –Impossible |
| 7:40PM – 7:50PM | Facilitated discussion of Daily Journal from the Book-Pages 199 – 201 | Constance Holmes | Slides 8-14 as each is being discussed |
| 7:50PM – 7:55PM | Summary of Bible Service | Dr. Ronald Holmes | Slide 15 and 16 |
| 7:55PM – 8:00PM | Closing Comments & Prayer | Reverend Frederick Newbill | Continue with Slide 16 |

*A 12 Week Bible Study from the Devotional Book "Beyond the Sunday Sermon"*

# WEEK 1: Visual Slides

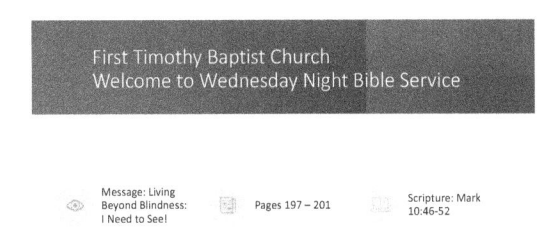

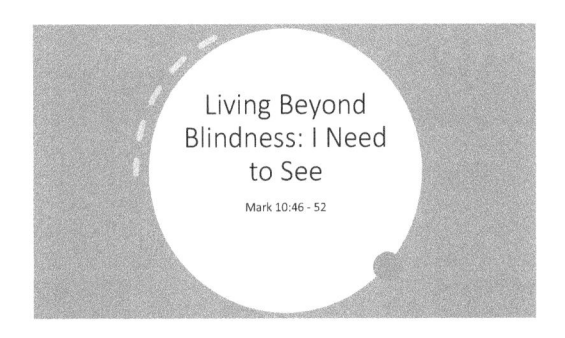

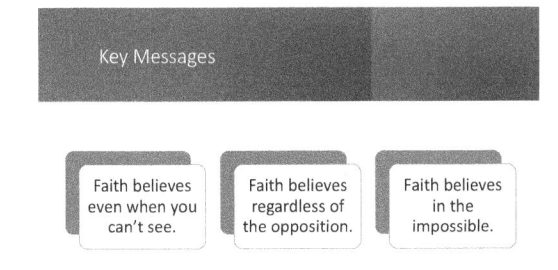

First Timothy Baptist Church
Welcome to Wednesday Night Bible Service

Message: Living Beyond Blindness: I Need to See!

Pages 197 – 201

Scripture: Mark 10:46-52

Living Beyond Blindness: I Need to See

Mark 10:46 - 52

Key Messages

- Faith believes even when you can't see.
- Faith believes regardless of the opposition.
- Faith believes in the impossible.

I will walk by faith, even when I can not see.

Faith believes even when you can't see.

Faith believes regardless of opposition.

Faith believes in the impossible.

Journal Discussion:

Living Beyond Blindness: I Need to See

*A 12 Week Bible Study from the Devotional Book "Beyond the Sunday Sermon"*

Question 1: What is the power of Prayer?

Question 2: Describe your faith in the Lord.

Question 3: As a Christian, discuss how you "walk by faith and not by sight."

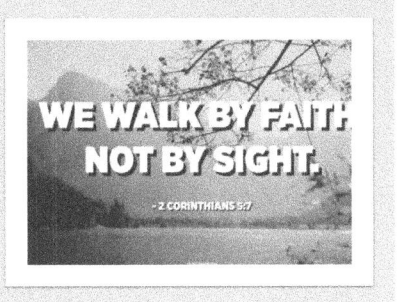

WE WALK BY FAITH NOT BY SIGHT.
- 2 CORINTHIANS 5:7

...He is a rewarder of them that diligently seek him.
Hebrews 11:6

Question 4: How has the Lord been a rewarder of your life as you diligently sought Him?

Question 5: Discuss some of the blessings the Lord has provided you because of your faith in Him.

Question 6: How has the Lord been the "bread of life" in your household for believing in Him?

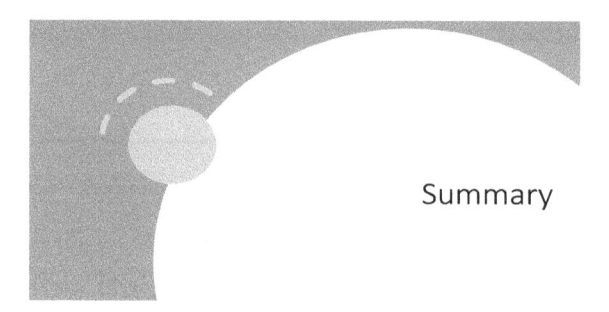

Summary

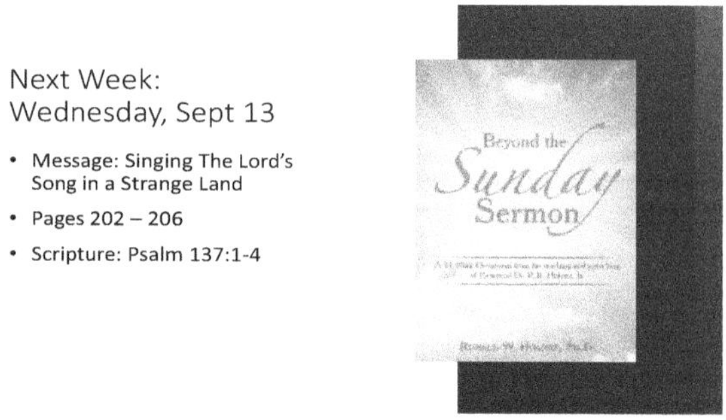

Next Week:
Wednesday, Sept 13

- Message: Singing The Lord's Song in a Strange Land
- Pages 202 – 206
- Scripture: Psalm 137:1-4

# WEEK 2

# Singing The Lord's Song in A Strange Land

"The mind is a terrible thing to waste," is a popular slogan used by the United Negro College Fund. The meaning of this quote is that our life is a reflection of our thoughts. We are driven by our thoughts; and our thoughts are driven by our mind. Our mind decides or controls everything in our life. In fact, we become what we feed to our mind according to Arthur Fletcher, the father of affirmative action.

Good evening, Reverend Newbill, members, friends, and guests of First Timothy Baptist Church's Wednesday Night Bible Service. We are happy to have you in person and online. Using our teaching style for this bible service, we are going to (1) read an excerpt of the Sunday Sermon and Scripture from the book titled *Beyond the Sunday Sermon*; (2) discuss the three key points from the Sunday Sermon lesson; (3) provide concrete details to support the key points; and (4) summarize the lesson with scriptures and questions from the daily journal.

At this time, Constance Holmes will come and read the excerpt of the lesson and scripture. Afterwards, I will highlight the three key points for the lesson on Singing the Lord's Song in A Strange Land.

Thank you, Constance, for reading the excerpts of the lesson and scripture. Now, let's look at the three key points about the behaviors of the Israelites for the lesson (1) the Israelites sat down by the rivers of Babylon; (2) the Israelites wept by the rivers of Babylon; and (3) the Israelites remembered Zion by the rivers of Babylon (Psalm 137: 1).

## Key Point 1:

The Israelites sat down by the rivers of Babylon. They were attacked by the Babylonians and carried away as captives from their home of Jerusalem to Babylon as caused by God for their disobedience to him (Jeremiah 29:4).

In 1619, our ancestors were carried away as captives from the shores of Africa. While in captivity, they built America and nurtured their minds with spiritual songs such as *Wade in the Water*; *Swing Low, Sweet Chariot*; and *Certainly Lord*.

While in captivity, the Israelites were told to build houses, start businesses, and raise families (Jeremiah 29: 5-6). In their minds, they questioned how they could sing the Lord's song while being in a strange land (Psalm 137:4). Have you ever been in a strange relationship and your mind could not take it anymore? Have you ever sat down on a job and refused to complete the work? Was there anything corrupting your mind to behave in such a manner? As mentioned earlier, our mind decides or controls everything in our life. We become what we feed our mind. When people are bullied and disrespected in a relationship or workplace, they sometimes allow their thoughts about the mistreatment to contaminate their mind. We can't let anything contaminate our mind and cause us to sit idly by and stop worshiping the Lord. In the song lyrics of Otis Redding, we can't just "sit on the dock of the bay and watch the tide roll away." We must redirect our mind, hold our peace, and allow the Lord to fight for us as noted in Exodus 14: 14.

## Key Point 2:

Secondly, the Israelites wept by the rivers of Babylon. Have you ever wept about something in your life? In this world, we got to weep sometimes. The bible teaches us that "weeping may endure for a night, but joy cometh in the morning" (Psalm 30: 5). When we are troubled by things in our life, we must keep the faith; and "calleth those things which be not as though they were" (Romans 4:17). We must feed our mind with the things the Lord has commanded us; and he will always be with us until the end of the world (Matthew 28: 20). We must also recognize the power of the Lord; and remember even in our weakness we still have him as illustrated in a song by Smokie Norful. Take a listen to the song.

## Key Point 3:

Thirdly, the Israelites remembered Zion by the rivers of Babylon because "there is no place like home." Ask Dorothy in the Wizard of Oz? The Israelites probably remembered the positive relationships they had with the Lord, and the many blessings they received from him such as good shelter, health, and wealth. The Israelites regretted being in a strange land just like the prodigal son regretted being in a strange land and wanted to go home (Luke 15: 11- 20).

However, the Israelites apparently had lost their religion and could not see how they could sing the Lord's songs in a strange land (Psalm 137:4). They hung their harps, put down their instruments and threw in the towel so to speak (Psalm 137:2). They were so concerned about their earthly conditions of being carried into captivity that they stopped praising the Lord (Psalm 137:3). They fell right into the trap of Satan who delights in taking advantage of you and stopping you from praising the Lord (2 Corinthians 2:11).

When do we remember the Lord? Is it when everything is going right in our life? Is it when we are faced with tribulations? Or is it a combination of both? We must remember to "trust the Lord with all our heart; and lean not unto our own understanding. In all our ways acknowledge him, and he shall direct our paths" (Proverbs 3: 5).

When we stop trusting, praising, worshiping, and remembering the goodness of the Lord, we start consuming our mind with other things that distract us from God's peace, grace, and mercy. We must remember God's grace is sufficient and He is all we need when we are weak (2 Corinthians 12: 9). We must remember God's goodness, love, and faithfulness as illustrated in a song by Nathaniel Bassey. Take a listen to the song.

In summary, the Israelites sat down, wept, and remembered Zion during their captivity by the rivers of Babylon (Psalm 137:1); and they could not sing the Lord's song in a strange land. Just like our ancestors who were carried away as captives from the shores of Africa, we must "serve the Lord with gladness: and come before his presence with singing"

(Psalms 100: 2). We must love the Lord with all our heart, soul, and mind (Mathew 22:37).

At this time, let's reflect on some of the daily journal questions from the book such as: What does it mean to "let the word of Christ dwell in you richly in all wisdom?" Constance will lead the discussion by first reading the scripture for a question and then providing her personal reflection to the question. She will be followed by others who would like to share their reflections to the questions as well.

We are now at the end of the bible service. I hope you have gained something from this service. I look forward to your participation in next Wednesday's lesson, titled Never Say Die (Pages 213– 218). The scripture is 2 Kings 7: 3 – 8. Please feel free to invite a guest to join us at the church or online; and spread the word about the service through social media platforms such as Facebook, Tik Tok, Twitter, Instagram, and LinkedIn. If anyone would like to purchase the book titled, *Beyond the Sunday Sermon*, you can order it online from Amazon.com, Barnes & Noble, or Authorhouse.

Now, we will have closing remarks from our pastor, Reverend Newbill.

*Ronald W. Holmes, Ph.D.*

# WEEK 2: Outline of Service

Outline of Service
First Timothy Wednesday Night Bible Service
September 13, 2023
7:00PM – 8:00PM

Message: Singing the Lord's Song in a Strange Land
from the book *"Beyond the Sunday Sermon"* (Pages 202 - 206)
Scripture: Psalm 137:1-4 KJV

| Time | What | By Whom | Music to play or Visual to Display |
|---|---|---|---|
| 6:53PM – 7:00PM | Song: I'll Just Say Yes by Brian Courtney Wilson (7:01) | Media Ministry to play song | • Play music – I'll Just Say Yes |
| 7:00PM – 7:03PM | Song: Music Video: Rivers of Babylon, Boney M. (3:29) | Media Ministry to play music video | • Play music video/ song – Rivers of Babylon |
| 7:03PM -7:05PM | Prayer and Intro of Wednesday Night Bible Service | Reverend Frederick Newbill | • Show Slide 1 – Singing the Lord's song in a strange land |
| 7:05PM – 7:10PM | Intro & Teaching Method | Dr. Ronald Holmes | • Show Slide 2 – A mind is a dangerous thing to waste |
| 7:10PM  7:13PM | Reading the Excerpt of Sunday Sermon & Scripture | Constance Holmes | • Slide 3 – Welcome to First Timothy- Wednesday Night Bible Study |
| 7:13PM – 7:20PM | • Three Key Points from the Message<br>• Supporting Details from the Message | Dr. Ronald Holmes | • Slide 4 - Key Messages |
| 7:20PM –7:24PM | Song:<br>• I Still Have You – Smokie Norful (4:14) | Media Ministry to play music video | • Slide 5 to show until Music Video Starts Playing<br>• Play music video/ song –I Still Have You |

| | | | |
|---|---|---|---|
| 7:24PM –7:27PM | Continue with Key Point Message #3 | | • Slide 6 - Key Messages |
| 7:27PM –7:29PM | Song/Video: I Remember – Nathaniel Bassey (only play up to 2:20 when it says, na,na,na) | Media Ministry to play music video | • Slide 7 to show until Music Video starts<br>• Play music video/ song –I Remember |
| 7:29PM – 7:50PM | Facilitated discussion of Daily Journal from the Book-Pages 204-206 | Constance Holmes | Slides 8-13 as each is being discussed |
| 7:50PM – 7:55PM | Summary of Bible Service | Dr. Ronald Holmes | Slide 14 and 15 |
| 7:55PM – 8:00PM | Closing Comments & Prayer | Reverend Frederick Newbill | Continue with Slide 15 |

- I'll Just Say Yes- https://youtu.be/_xPbESClUDg?si=05esMLCb5CMDiQQe
- Rivers of Babylon - https://www.youtube.com/watch?v=2FgDles4xq8&pp=ygUbQm9uZXkgTS4gLVJpdmVycyBvZiBCYWJ5bG9u
- I Still Have You - https://www.youtube.com/watch?v=lT7tSjPb5dA&pp=ygUhc21va2llIG5vcmZ1bCAtIGkgc3RpbGwgaGF2ZSB5b3Ug

I Remember - https://www.youtube.com/watch?v=jAA-sEEkURk

Ronald W. Holmes, Ph.D.

# WEEK 2: Visual Slides

**Singing the Lord's song in a strange land**
Pages 202 – 206

*A Mind is a Terrible Thing to Waste*
ARTHUR FLETCHER, UNITED NEGRO COLLEGE FUND

**WELCOME TO FIRST TIMOTHY** KJV
Wednesday Night Bible Service
HOLY BIBLE

| KEY MESSAGES ABOUT THE ISRAELITES |
|---|

| …Sat down by the rivers of Babylon | …Wept by the rivers of Babylon. | …Remembered Zion |
|---|---|---|

18

*A 12 Week Bible Study from the Devotional Book "Beyond the Sunday Sermon"*

SMOKIE NORFUL

NATHANIEL BASSEY

### KEY MESSAGES ABOUT THE ISRAELITES

- ...Sat down by the rivers of Babylon
- ...Wept by the rivers of Babylon.
- ...Remembered Zion

### JOURNAL DISCUSSION:

### SINGING THE LORD'S SONG IN A STRANGE LAND

WHAT SONGS DO YOU SING TO PRAISE THE LORD?

WHAT DOES IT MEAN TO "LET THE WORD OF CHRIST DWELL IN YOU RICHLY IN ALL WISDOM?"

AS A CHRISTIAN, WHAT ARE THE BENEFITS OF REJOICING AND SINGING PRAISES TO THE LORD?

HOW HAS THE LORD BEEN YOUR "DEFENSE AND REFUGE IN THE DAY OF TROUBLE?"

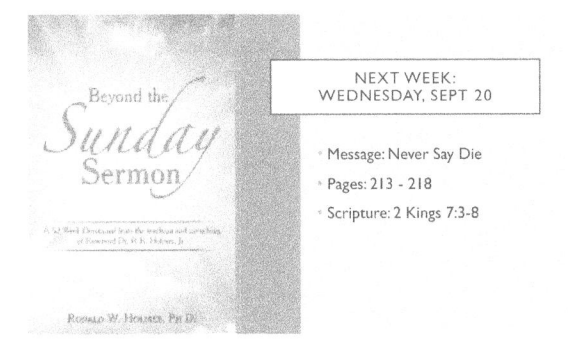

*A 12 Week Bible Study from the Devotional Book "Beyond the Sunday Sermon"*

# SUMMARY

**NEXT WEEK:
WEDNESDAY, SEPT 20**

- Message: Never Say Die
- Pages: 213 - 218
- Scripture: 2 Kings 7:3-8

# WEEK 3

# Never Say Die

Good evening, Reverend Milton, members, friends, and guest of First Timothy Baptist Church's Wednesday Night Bible Service. On behalf of our pastor Fredrick Newbill, we are happy to have you today in church and online for the lesson on "Never Say Die." When I think about this lesson, I think about my experience as a student athlete.

For example, I was told that a winner never quits, and a quitter never wins. I was told that you might bend but you don't break. I was told that the race is won not by the fastest, but to the one who endures to the end. I was told that through blood, sweat and tears, you finish the task regardless of the hurdles; and I was told that you "Never Say Die" or quit anything in life. Rather, you keep hope alive because the best is yet to come when you know Jesus as your Lord and Savior.

Using our teaching style for this bible service, we are going to (1) read an excerpt of the Sunday Sermon and Scripture from the book titled *"Beyond the Sunday Sermon;"* (2) discuss the three key points from the Sunday Sermon lesson; (3) provide concrete details to support the key points; and (4) summarize the lesson with scriptures and questions from the daily

journal. At this time, Constance Holmes will come and read the excerpt of the lesson and scripture.

Thank you, Constance, for reading the excerpt of the lesson and scripture. Now, let's look at the three key points about the lepers' situation to current events. The lesson will focus on (1) a conversation and retreat; (2) the calculation to remain; and (3) the courage over risk.

## Key Point 1:

Just like the conversations of the lepers contemplating over their choices for survival in 2 Kings: 7: 4, many family members, loved ones, and friends had conversations about their choices of survival in taking the COVID-19 vaccine or doing absolutely nothing and possibly dying. This American problem got so bad that I wrote an open letter to the public. I reminded the people in the community that as a child, you were vaccinated for the measles, mumps, and chickenpox. You got a shot before you started school for pre-K and elementary. While your body never had a negative reaction from these medications, the critical questions to be asked are: Why won't you get vaccinated? How long do you want this war on COVID-19 to last? Do you prefer to retreat from taking the vaccine that can possibly save your life and protect the lives of other people in your community?

In military terms, the vaccine is our weapon to fight the enemy. The vaccine is equipped with the latest artillery and technology to win the war on COVID-19. This war, however, requires every soldier regardless of race, sex, religion, class, party affiliation or nationality to arm himself or herself with the vaccine. The reason is clear. The enemy is a dangerous disease that spreads from person to person.

Despite efforts from the media, preachers, community leaders, doctors, and the president of the U.S., many people chose to do nothing and, subsequently, died from the virus. We must be reminded that in this world we are going to have trials and tribulations; but be of good cheer. Jesus has overcome the world (John 16:33). Considering the health condition of the four lepers, they were put out of society because of leprosy and there was no cure or vaccine for it; they were going to die from this disease or hunger. If they went into the city, they would be killed. They were excommunicated. They had no legal and medical rights. However, the lepers did not retreat. They conversed over their choices (2 Kings: 7: 4) and decided to go to the camp of the Syrians (2 Kings: 7: 5). Perhaps, they had a "Job" type mentality. When he said, yet he slay me, I still will trust in him (Job 13:15). This verse is highlighted in a song by the Mississippi Mass Choir. Take a Listen to the song.

## Key Point 2:

Secondly, the lepers assessed the calculation to remain sitting idle during their state of sickness. Instead of sitting down, weeping, and remembering their home like the Israelites on the rivers of Babylon, the lepers raised the critical question, "Why sit we here until we die?" (2 Kings 7: 3). They rationalized their choices (2 Kings 7: 4). They realized that sitting was not going to make them well but would lead to their immediate death. This was not the case for the people in the U.S. While dying in the hospital from COVID-19, many people stated they wished they had taken the vaccine to save their lives. Perhaps, time was of essence for the lepers, so they decided the best course of action for them. Perhaps, they realized that the Lord said, I'm going to do a new thing even in the wilderness (Isaiah 43: 19).

**Key Point 3:**

Thirdly, many people such as Martin Luther King Jr. and Rosa Parks displayed courage over risk of their lives to make the world a better place to live. Considering the risk of dying, the four lepers entered the camp of Syrians, found the Syrians had fled from the place, and left all their goods, possessions, and belongings. This miracle was through the grace of God who allowed the lepers' courage over risk to become a blessing to them (2 Kings 7: 5-8). I can hear one of the lepers saying, (using some of the words from a song by Pastor Mike Jr.), "I remember when, I remember when, he saved my life. I am a living witness that my God is amazing. The truth is I should be crazy; I think God, he saved me. I could have died last year;" but I am still here. "Now I can testify; I'll never be the same." God changed my name. "I'm alive. I survived." What didn't kill me from hunger, it only made me stronger. God kept me from the midst of it all; when I was facing turmoil. Now, take a Listen to the song by Pastor Mike Jr.

In summary, First Timothy, the lepers, and people in the U.S. had conversations about their livelihood. They assessed the calculation to remain sitting idle during their state of illness. While the lepers displayed the courage over risk to enter the camp of the Syrians, many Americans chose to do nothing and subsequently died from COVID-19. The bible reminds us that we are going to have trials and tribulations, but be of good cheer. Jesus our Lord and Savior has overcome the world (John 16:33). Amen.

At this time, let's reflect on some of the daily journal questions from the book, "Beyond the Sunday Sermon." Constance will lead the discussion.

We are now at the end of the bible service. I hope you have gained something from this service. I look forward to your participation in next

Wednesday's lesson, titled The Gift of Prayer (Pages 219 - 224). The scripture is Hebrews 4:14 -16. Please feel free to invite a guest to join us at the church or online; and spread the word about the service through social media platforms such as Facebook, Tik Tok, Twitter, Instagram, and LinkedIn. If anyone would like to purchase the book, *"Beyond the Sunday Sermon,"* you can order it online from Amazon.com, Barnes & Noble, or Authorhouse.

Now, we will have closing remarks from Minister Milton.

*A 12 Week Bible Study from the Devotional Book "Beyond the Sunday Sermon"*

# WEEK 3: Outline of Service

Outline of Service
First Timothy Wednesday Night Bible Service
September 20, 2023
7:00PM – 8:00PM

Message: Never Say Die
from the book *"Beyond the Sunday Sermon"* (Pages 213- 218)
Scripture: 2 Kings 7:3-8 KJV

| Time | What | By Whom | Music to play or Visual to Display |
|---|---|---|---|
| 6:53PM – 7:00PM | Song/video: I'll Just Say Yes by Brian Courtney Wilson (7:01) | Media Ministry to play song/ video | • Play song/music – I'll Just Say Yes |
| 7:00PM -7:05PM | Prayer and Intro of Wednesday Night Bible Service | Minister Jonas Milton | • Show Slide 1 – Never Say Die |
| 7:05PM – 7:10PM | Intro & Teaching Method | Dr. Ronald Holmes | • Show Slide 2 then 3 – Welcome/Ronald, the student athlete |
| 7:10PM – 7:13PM | Reading the Excerpt of Sunday Sermon & Scripture | Constance Holmes | • Slide 4 – Lessons from 4 Lepers |
| 7:13PM – 7:18PM | • Three Key Points from the Message<br>• Supporting Details from the Message | Dr. Ronald Holmes | • Slide 5 & 6 - Key Messages |
| 7:18PM –7:23PM | Song/Video:<br>• Trust in the Lord - Mississippi Mass Choir - (5:11) | Media Ministry to play music video | • Slide 7 to show until Music Video Starts Playing<br>• Play music video/ song –Trust in the Lord |
| 7:23PM –7:28PM | • Continue with Key Point Message 2 & 3 | Dr. Ronald Holmes | • Slide 8 - Key Messages 2&3 |
| 7:28PM –7:31PM | Song/Video: Amazing – Pastor Mike Jr. (3:27) | Media Ministry to play music video | • Slide 9 to show until Music Video starts<br>• Play music video/ song –Amazing |

| 7:31PM – 7:50PM | Facilitated discussion of Daily Journal from the Book- Pages 216-218 | Constance Holmes | • Slides 10-14 as each is being discussed |
| 7:50PM – 7:55PM | Summary of Bible Service | Dr. Ronald Holmes | • Slide 15 & 16 |
| 7:55PM – 8:00PM | Closing Comments & Prayer | Minister Jonas Milton | • Continue with Slide 16 |

- I'll Just Say Yes- https://www.youtube.com/watch?v=mZ_sMqDYWj8
- Trust in the Lord – https://youtu.be/7nJQD4L3aLA?si=gtCPpiChsln_d54j
- Amazing - https://youtu.be/JsE_IxOg72c?si=xA7HgtQh675oW-LV

*A 12 Week Bible Study from the Devotional Book "Beyond the Sunday Sermon"*

# WEEK 3: Visual Slides

*Ronald W. Holmes, Ph.D.*

## KEY MESSAGES ABOUT THE LEPERS

- ...Conversation to Retreat
- ...The calculation to remain
- ...Courage over risk

MISSISSIPPI MASS CHOIR

AMAZING PASTOR MIKE JR.

*A 12 Week Bible Study from the Devotional Book "Beyond the Sunday Sermon"*

### KEY MESSAGES ABOUT THE LEPERS

- ...Conversation to Retreat
- ...The calculation to remain
- ...Courage over risk

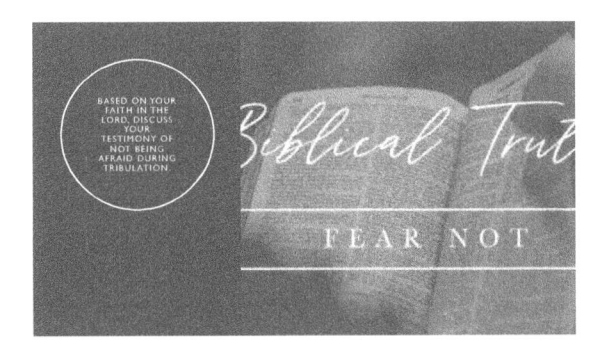

**JOURNAL DISCUSSION:**

**NEVER SAY DIE**

DISCUSS HOW YOU HAVE BEEN BLESSED BY GOD BECAUSE OF YOUR BELIEF IN HIM.

BASED ON YOUR FAITH IN THE LORD, DISCUSS YOUR TESTIMONY OF NOT BEING AFRAID DURING TRIBULATION.

*Biblical Truth*

FEAR NOT

Ronald W. Holmes, Ph.D.

DESCRIBE HOW YOU HAVE WITNESSED THE BLESSING OF GOD THROUGH DIFFICULT SITUATIONS

DISCUSS AN EXPERIENCE IN YOUR LIFE THAT APPEARED TO BE IMPOSSIBLE BUT WAS POSSIBLE THROUGH THE GRACE OF GOD

SUMMARY

Wednesday Bible Study 9/27

The Gift of Prayer
Pages 219 – 224
Hebrews 4:14 - 16

# WEEK 4

# The Gift of Prayer

This is the day the Lord has made. Let us rejoice and be glad in it. Good evening, Reverend Newbill, members, friends, and guest of First Timothy Baptist Church's Wednesday Night Bible Study. We are happy to have you today in church and online for the lesson on "The Gift of Prayer."

As a child, my mama told me to read my bible; she did not tell me to knock you out as rapper LL Cool J conveys in his song (Mama said knock you out – I'm going to knock you out). No sir! No ma'am! My mama told me to read my bible. She had a divine purpose in mind; so at the end of the year 2021, I made the commitment to read and study intensely my bible and write the Book, *"Beyond the Sunday Sermon."* The impact of mama's purpose for me to read my bible came to fruition. She knew that the bible says in Proverbs 22: 6, "Train up a child in the way he should go: and when he is old, he will not depart from it." I didn't depart from it!

Using our teaching style for this bible study, we are going to (1) read an excerpt of the Sunday Sermon and Scripture from the book titled *"Beyond the Sunday Sermon;"* (2) discuss the three key points from the Sunday Sermon lesson; (3) provide concrete details to support the key points; and (4) summarize the lesson with scriptures and questions from the daily

journal. At this time, Constance Holmes will come and read the excerpt of the lesson and scripture.

Thank you, Constance. Now, let's look closely at the three key points about the significance of the gift of prayer available to all humankind. The focus of the lesson includes (1) the priesthood of Christ; (2) the preeminence of Christ; and (3) the provision of Christ.

## Key Point 1:

We have a great high priest in Jesus who has passed through the heavens and is the son of God (Hebrews 4:14). He has given us a gift of salvation, eternal life, and the Holy Spirit. He has given us the fruit of the Spirit, spiritual gifts, and the gift of prayer to help us to navigate through life's burdens, conflicts, disappointments, and hardships.

Jesus instructs us (men and women) to always "pray and not to faint" (Luke 18:1); and when we pray say, "Our Father which art in heaven, Hallowed be thy name. Thy kingdom come. Thy will be done in earth, as it is in heaven" (Matthew 6: 9-10). Jesus prayed on the mountain before his crucifixion, so we must follow Jesus and pray for our oppression. We must hold fast to our profession (Hebrews 4:14). This means to hold fast to our confession of faith; or hold fast to our belief in Jesus.

How do you know? I'm glad you asked the question. In Romans 10:9, the bible says, "If thou shalt confess with thy mouth the Lord Jesus, and shalt believe in thine heart that God hath raised him from the dead, thou shalt be saved."

Jesus, our great high priest, came to be with us, not forsake us as written in Matthew 1:23. "Behold, a virgin shall be with child, and shall bring forth a son, and they shall call his name Emmanuel, which being interpreted, God with us" (Hebrews 10:23).

Jesus, our great high priest, is on the right hand of God interceding for us when we are sad, depressed, broken, worried, or frustrated (Romans 8:34). We must be steadfast in our prayer (Hebrews 10:13), hold fast to our confession of faith, and believe that Jesus can answer our prayers when petitioned. Do I have a witness? Do you believe that Jesus will answer our prayers? Yes, I'm glad you responded correctly because the bible says in St. Matthew 21:22, "And all things whatsoever ye shall ask in prayer, believing, ye shall receive."

Jesus, our great high priest, is the risen Christ. He is no ordinary priest. Pastors, Bishops, and others will depart from here; but Christ is a priest forever. We must draw near to him and he will draw near to us (James 4:8).

This is illustrated in a song titled *"Draw Me Nearer."* Some of the words to the song are: I'm thine oh Lord. I have heard thy voice, and it told thy love to me. But I long to rise, in the arms of faith; and be closer drawn to thee. Draw me nearer, nearer blessed Lord, to the cross where thou hast died. Draw me nearer, nearer blessed Lord, to thy precious, bleeding side. Consecrate me now to thy service, Lord, by the power of grace divine. Let my soul look up with a steadfast hope, and my will be lost in thine. Draw me nearer, nearer blessed Lord, to the cross where thou hast died. Draw me nearer, nearer blessed Lord, to the precious, bleeding side. Now, take a listen to this song by BeKofi.

## Key Point 2:

Secondly, the preeminence of Christ is that we have a great high priest who is superior and first in everything. He carried our burdens, was wounded for our transgressions, and bruised for our iniquities (Isaiah 53:5). We have a great high priest who can be touched with a feeling of our infirmities (Hebrews 4:15). Jesus feels what we feel and hurts when we hurt. Our pain is His pain. He is always available to hear our concerns as recorded in Philippians 4: 6-7. This was not the case when I was in graduate school. Some professors were too busy to hear our concerns regarding an assignment. In fact, you could not see them unless you had an appointment. They wanted to tempt us and see how much we could bare.

I'm so happy that Jesus knows how much we can bare. He was "tempted like as we are, yet without sin" (Hebrews 4:15). He took our sins and nailed them to the cross. He was born to save us from our sins. Where is your proof? I'm glad you asked the question. Let me refer you to Matthew 1:21: It reads: "And she shall bring forth a son, and thou shalt call his name Jesus: for he shall save his people from their sins." Okay, that is good; but how do we escape our sins from being tempted? I'm glad you asked that question too. Let me refer you to 1 Corinthians 10: 13: It reads: "God is faithful, who will not suffer you to be tempted above that ye are able; but will with the temptation also make a way to escape, that ye may be able to bear it."

This is the reason we "Never Say Die" as noted in bible study last week. We must keep hope alive because the best is yet to come through Jesus as our Lord and Savior. We can do all things through Christ who strengthens us (Philippians 4: 13).

## Key Point 3:

Finally, as a spiritual provision, God promises to supply all our needs as recorded in Philippians 4:19. The scripture in (Hebrews 4:16) reads, "Let us therefore come boldly unto the throne of grace." If we do so, First Timothy, what will happen when we get there? I'm glad you asked the question. The bible says in Hebrews 4:16, "that we may obtain mercy, and find grace to help in time of need."

"Let us come boldly," not timidly "unto the throne of grace." We come boldly because we are believers of Jesus Christ. We come boldly because of what he did at the cross. He said, "It is finished" before he died for our sins (John 19:30). We come boldly because Jesus conquered death and prepared a place for us. We come boldly because Jesus said I'm coming. I came the first time. I'm coming again (John 14:3).

Therefore, we must be prepared for his return. Using some of the words in a song by Jekalyn Carr called *"Jehovah Jireh,"* we must believe as our faith is tested. We must have the faith that God will come through like he did for Abraham. He will show us a sign during manifestation time. We must have the faith that God will not let us down. He will always be around. He is the alpha and omega. He the beginning and the ending. He the same God today and yesterday. He raised Lazarus from the dead. He gives us peace so we can rest comfortably in our bed. He delivered the three Hebrew boys. He will provide for all our chores. He is Jehovah Jireh. I won't stop believing because he is my path for survival. Now, take a listen to this song by Jekalyn Carr.

In summary, First Timothy, we have a great high priest in Jesus who has given us the gift of prayer to help us to navigate through life's burdens.

Jesus is superior and first in everything. He will supply all our needs. We must thank him for his grace and mercy. Amen.

At this time, let's reflect on some of the daily journal questions on prayer from the book, "Beyond the Sunday Sermon." Constance will lead the discussion.

We are now at the end of bible study. We hope you have gained something from this bible study. We look forward to your participation in next Wednesday's lesson titled Believe the Promise (Pages 225 - 230) from the book *"Beyond the Sunday Sermon."* The scripture is Romans 8:28.

Now, we will have closing remarks from Reverend Newbill.

*A 12 Week Bible Study from the Devotional Book "Beyond the Sunday Sermon"*

# WEEK 4: Outline of Service

Outline of Service
First Timothy Wednesday Night Bible Service
September 27, 2023
7:00PM – 8:00PM

Message: The Gift of Prayer
from the book *"Beyond the Sunday Sermon"* (Pages 219- 230)
Scripture: Hebrews 4:14-16 KJV

| Time | What | By Whom | Music to play or Visual to Display |
|---|---|---|---|
| 6:53PM – 7:00PM | Song/video: I'll Just Say Yes by Brian Courtney Wilson (7:01) | Media Ministry to play song/video | • Play song/music – I'll Just Say Yes |
| 7:00PM -7:05PM | Prayer and Intro of Wednesday Night Bible Service | Reverend Frederick Newbill | • Show Slide 1 – Wednesday Night Bible Study |
| 7:05PM – 7:10PM | Intro & Teaching Method | Dr. Ronald Holmes | • Show Slide 2 then 3 – Welcome/Ronald |
| 7:10PM – 7:13PM | Reading the Excerpt of Sunday Sermon & Scripture | Constance Holmes | • Slide 4 – The Gift of Prayer |
| 7:13PM – 7:18PM | • Three Key Points from the Message<br>• Supporting Details from the Message | Dr. Ronald Holmes | • Slide 5 - Key Messages |
| 7:18PM –7:23PM | Song/Video:<br>• I am Thine O Lord - (5:45) - BeKofi | Media Ministry to play music video | • Slide 6 to show until Music Video Starts Playing<br>• Play music video/ song –I am Thine O Lord |
| 7:23PM –7:28PM | • Continue with Key Point Message 2 & 3 | Dr. Ronald Holmes | • Slide 7 - Key Messages 2&3 |
| 7:28PM –7:32PM | Song/Video: Jehovah Jireh –(Play until 4:31) Jekalyn Carr | Media Ministry to play music video | • Slide 8 to show until Music Video starts<br>• Play music video/ song –Jehovah Jireh |

| 7:32PM – 7:50PM | Facilitated discussion of Daily Journal from the Book- Pages 222-224 | Constance Holmes | • Slides 9-13 as each is being discussed |
| --- | --- | --- | --- |
| 7:50PM – 7:55PM | Summary of Bible Service | Dr. Ronald Holmes | • Slide 14 & 15 |
| 7:55PM – 8:00PM | Closing Comments & Prayer | Reverend Frederick Newbill | • Continue with Slide 15 |

- I'll Just Say Yes- https://www.youtube.com/watch?v=mZ_sMqDYWj8
- I Am Thine O Lord – https://youtu.be/5pV7rzS2o1o?si=65sL3N2korHC-C9w
- Jehovah Jireh- https://youtu.be/Yjey4J2b5Rs?si=B8_AFtYx68WES0v

*A 12 Week Bible Study from the Devotional Book "Beyond the Sunday Sermon"*

# WEEK 4: Visual Slides

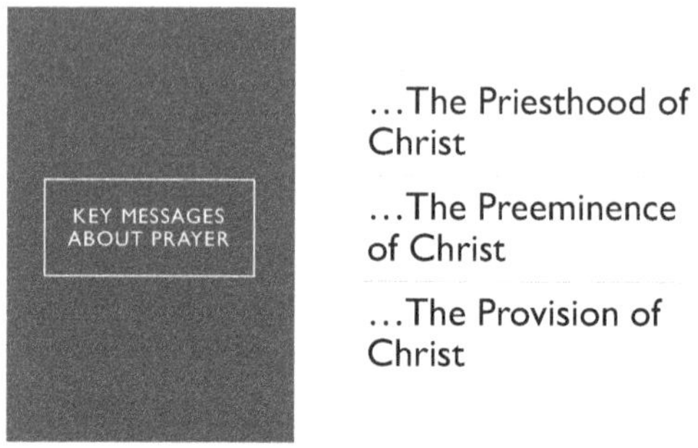

**KEY MESSAGES ABOUT PRAYER**

...The Priesthood of Christ

...The Preeminence of Christ

...The Provision of Christ

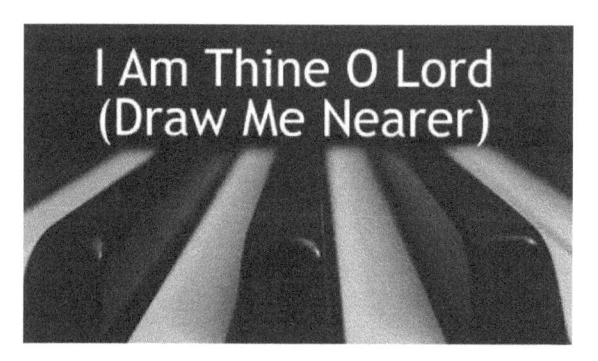

**I Am Thine O Lord (Draw Me Nearer)**

Jekalyn Carr
Jehovah Jireh

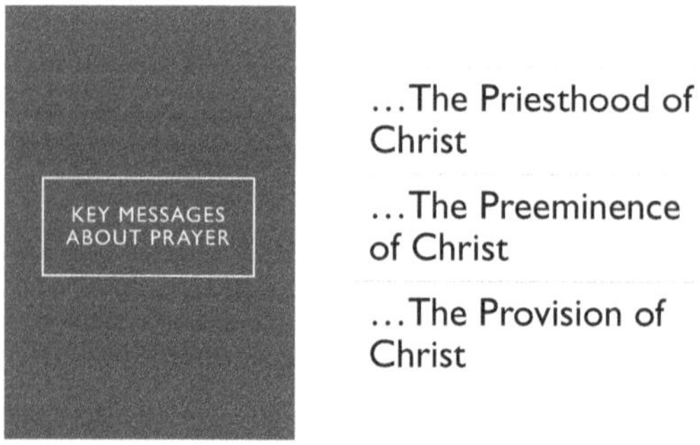

**KEY MESSAGES ABOUT PRAYER**

...The Priesthood of Christ

...The Preeminence of Christ

...The Provision of Christ

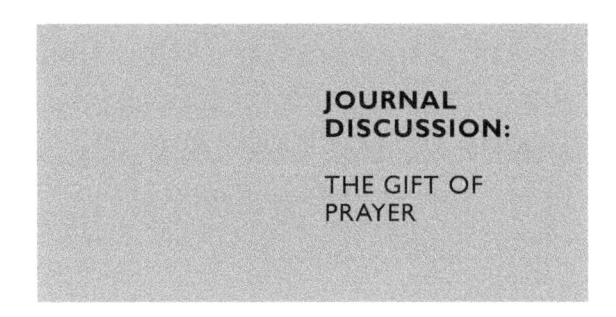

*A 12 Week Bible Study from the Devotional Book "Beyond the Sunday Sermon"*

**JOURNAL DISCUSSION:**

THE GIFT OF PRAYER

**PRAYER AND EXPECTATION**

WHAT IS YOUR EXPECTATION OF PRAYER

**BE CAREFUL for nothing;**
but in every thing by prayer and supplication with thanksgiving let your requests be made known unto God
Philippians 4:6

Ask and it will be given to you
Seek and you will find
Knock and it will be opened to you
Matthew 7:7

*Ronald W. Holmes, Ph.D.*

> DISCUSS AN EXPERIENCE IN YOUR LIFE THAT THE LORD HEARD YOUR CRY AND DELIVERED YOU FROM A DIFFICULT SITUATION.

## SUMMARY

### BELIEVE THE PROMISE

PAGES 225 - 230

ROMANS 8:28

OCTOBER 4, 2023

WEEK 5

# Believe the Promise

Good evening, Reverend Newbill, members, friends, and guest of First Timothy Baptist Church's Wednesday Night Bible Study. We are happy to have you today in church and online for the lesson on "Believe the Promise."

In this world, we often make promises and keep those promises despite extenuating circumstances. Approximately, five weeks ago, I made the promise to Reverend Newbill to facilitate the relaunching of First Timothy's Wedneday Night Bible Study. I just said yes and I'm happy to do so; I'm equally happy that members of First Timothy bought into the promise and are playing an integral part of the bible study; and I want to thank you for your stewardship (Brothers Terrence, Green, & Brown and Sister Marsh). I want thank you First Timothy for your attendance, passion, participation, and commitment to the bible study. As we believe the promise of the Lord according to Romans 8:2, He will strengthen our lives.

Using our teaching style for this bible study, we are going to (1) read an excerpt of the Sunday Sermon and Scripture from the book titled Beyond the Sunday Sermon; (2) discuss the three key points from the Sunday

Sermon lesson; (3) provide concrete details to support the key points; and (4) summarize the lesson with scriptures and questions from the daily journal. At this time, Constance Holmes will come and read the excerpt of the lesson and scripture.

Thank you, Constance. Now, let's look closely at the three key points about the promise of the Lord as recorded in Romans 8:28. The lesson focuses on (1) the confidence of the promise; (2) the completeness of the promise; and (3) the condition of the promise.

## Key Point 1:

I would like to start this first key point on the confidence of the promise with a question. What is the promise for being saved? The bible says, "For whosoever shall call upon the name of the Lord shall be saved" (Romans 10:13). Once being saved and trusting in the Lord with all our heart, we must have the confidence of the promise to live by Romans 8:28. We must know that whatever we ask the Lord according to his will, he hears us. "And if we know that he hears us, whatsoever we ask, we know that we have the petitions that we desired of him" (1 John 5: 14-15). Additionally, when we are saved, we know that we are born again; "the Lord is my Shephard, I shall not want" (Psalms 23:1`). "The Lord is my light and my salvation whom shall I fear; the Lord is the strength of my life whom, shall I be afraid" (Psalm 27: 1). We know that "if God be for us, who can be against us" (Romans 8:31). We know that "God loveth a cheerful giver" (2 Corinthians 9: 7). "It's more blessed to give than to receive" (Acts 20:35).

I would like to share with you a story related to the confidence of the promise as written in Romans 8:28. Approximately, two hours before Wednesday Night Bible Study last week, I severely injured my hamstring attending to a dangerous snake on my premises. I had a big fall. In fact, Humpty Dumpty and all his great men could not put me back together again. The injury was so severe that my wife told me to get a substitute or throw in the towel so to speak. Before listening to her sincere comments, I petitioned the Lord to give me the strength to make it to bible study, complete my role with little or no pain, and go to the hospital thereafter. I had the confidence that the Lord heard my cry and would answer my prayer although I could not put my clothes on without assistance from my wife. I could neither stand nor walk. I could only crawl from the house to the back seat of my wife's car and into a wheelchair once I got to the church. God answered my prayer. What appeared to be impossible, the Lord made it possible for me to attend bible study.

Whenever we are dethroned, defeated, depressed, stressed or dealing with a dilemma, misfortune, mishap, or hardship, just remember the confidence of the promise that we know that all things work together for good to those who love God and are "called according to his purpose" (Romans 8:28).

We know that prayer changes things. I was not sure of my condition once I reached the hospital. After bible study, Sister Deeds immediately requested Minister Milton and others to assemble and pray for my health; and Minister Milton did such and prayed that I did not have any fractures from the injury as determined by the hospital. The bible says, "For where two or three are gathered together in my name, there am I in the midst of them" (Matthew 18:20).

Based on the X-rays at the hospital, the elder through faith, received a good report (Hebrews 11:2). I did not have any fractures from the injury. I want to thank you First Timothy for your petition and confidence in the promise and gift of prayer by our Lord and Savior Jesus Christ. Jesus is the answer for the world today. There is no other; Jesus is the way.

In trying to find a song that coincide with the message and the culture of First Timothy, I thought about singer Byron Cage in his song the presence, power, and spirit of the Lord is here; I can feel it in the atmosphere; but as I thought more about my health condition and how determined I was to keep the promise and come to bible study, I meditated on a song by Zacardi Cortez titled *"Lord Do It For Me."* Cortez indicates in the song, Lord if you don't do it for me, it won't get done. Take a listen to the song.

## Key Point 2:

Secondly, the completeness of the promise is that "all" things work together for the good of those who love the Lord (Romans 8:28). Not some things, a few things, a lot of things; good things or bad things but "all" things work together for the good of those who love the Lord. There is no exceptions or exemptions of what the Lord can do. The Lord can bring good from "all" situations. He can turn water into wine. Remember Jesus' first miracle at the wedding in Galilee. He can enable the blind to see. Remember blind Bartimaeus in Jericho. He can bring someone who is spiritually lost back home. Remember the Prodigal Son. Jesus can heal the sick. Remember the woman with the issue of blood who touched the hem of his garment. He can rescue people from a disease, starvation, and homelessness. Remember the four Lepers who went to the camp of the Syrians. What is the point? "With God, all things are possible" as recorded in Matthew 19: 26. Not a few things, some things, or a lot of things; but all things are possible. Therefore, we must put our faith, trust, and belief in the Lord.

## Key Point 3:

Thirdly, many universities accept students in school based on some condition. One example might require students to attend summer school at the university and pass all their classes before they are granted full acceptance at the university. The condition of the promise for God is very selective too. The promise is solely for God's people. It is predicated on those who love him and are called according to his purpose (Romans 8:28). Do you Love God? Do you know that God will answer your prayers? Do you know that what God has for you, is for you? Do you know that "greater is he that is in you than he that is in the world?" (1 John 4:4).

Do you know the song by Deborah Barnes that God will heal the land *If My People*, "which are called by my name, humble themselves and pray, and seek my face and turn from their wicked ways; then will I hear from heaven and will forgive their sin, and will heal their land" as recorded in 2 Chronicles 7:14. For meditation and edification, take a listen to the song *If My People* by Deborah Barnes.

In summary, First Timothy, we must be believers of the Lord and have the confidence of the promise to live by Romans 8:28. We must understand the completeness of the promise that all things work together for the good of those who love the Lord. We must also understand that the condition of the promise is very selective to those who love the Lord and are called according to His purpose. Amen.

At this time, let's reflect on some of the daily journal questions on promise from the book, "Beyond the Sunday Sermon." Constance will lead the discussion.

We are now at the end of bible study. We hope you have gained something from this bible study. We look forward to your participation in next Wednesday's lesson, titled Go Thy Way! Give God Thanks! (Pages 231 - 236) from the book *"Beyond the Sunday Sermon."* The scripture is: St. Luke 17: 11 – 19.

Now, we will have closing remarks from Reverend Newbill.

*A 12 Week Bible Study from the Devotional Book "Beyond the Sunday Sermon"*

# WEEK 5: Outline of Service

First Timothy Wednesday Night Bible Study
October 4, 2023
7:00PM – 8:00PM

Message: Believe the Promise
from the book *"Beyond the Sunday Sermon"* (Pages 225 - 230)
Scripture: Romans 8:28 KJV

| Time | What | By Whom | Music to play or Visual to Display |
|---|---|---|---|
| 6:53PM – 7:00PM | Song/video: I'll Just Say Yes by Brian Courtney Wilson (7:01) | Media Ministry to play song/video | • Play song/music – I'll Just Say Yes |
| 7:00PM -7:03PM | Prayer and Intro of Wednesday Night Bible Study | Reverend Frederick Newbill | • Show Slide 1 – Wednesday Night Bible Study |
| 7:03PM – 7:05PM | Intro, Thank You & Teaching Method | Dr. Ronald Holmes | • Show Slide 2 then 3 – Welcome/Ronald |
| 7:05PM – 7:10PM | Reading the Excerpt of Sunday Sermon & Scripture | Constance Holmes | • Slide 4 – Believe the Promise |
| 7:10PM – 7:18PM | • Three Key Points from the Message<br>• Supporting Details from the Message | Dr. Ronald Holmes | • Slide 5,6,7 - Key Messages |
| 7:18PM –7:25PM | Song/Video:<br>• Lord Do it For Me - (7:36) – Zacardi Cortez | Media Ministry to play music video | • Slide 8 to show until Music Video Starts Playing<br>• Play music video/song –Lord Do It For Me |
| 7:25PM –7:29PM | • Continue with Key Point Message 2 & 3 | Dr. Ronald Holmes | • Slide 9,10 - Key Messages 2&3 |
| 7:29PM –7:37PM | • Song/Video: If My People – (8:32) Deborah Barnes | Media Ministry to play music video | • Slide 11 to show until Music Video starts<br>• Play music video/song –If My People |

*Ronald W. Holmes, Ph.D.*

| 7:37PM – 7:38PM | • Summarize key points | Dr. Ronald Holmes | • Slide 12 – Summary of Key Points |
|---|---|---|---|
| 7:38PM – 7:50PM | Facilitated discussion of Daily Journal from the Book-Pages 228-230 | Constance Holmes | • Slides 13 -17- as each is being discussed |
| 7:50PM – 7:55PM | Summary of Bible Study | Dr. Ronald Holmes | • Slide 18 & 19 |
| 7:55PM – 8:00PM | Closing Comments & Prayer | Reverend Frederick Newbill | • Continue with Slide 19 |

- I'll Just Say Yes- https://www.youtube.com/watch?v=mZ_sMqDYWj8
- Lord Do It For Me – https://youtu.be/NszdPm11bP8
- If My People – https://youtu.be/Ug6fv8KRuCM?si=FfchOZ3cDhYIy4zQ

*A 12 Week Bible Study from the Devotional Book "Beyond the Sunday Sermon"*

# WEEK 5: Visual Slides

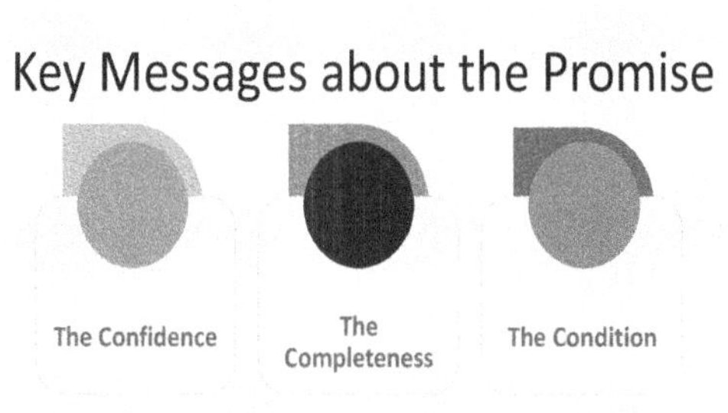

*Ronald W. Holmes, Ph.D.*

Zacardi Cortez
Lord, Do It For Me

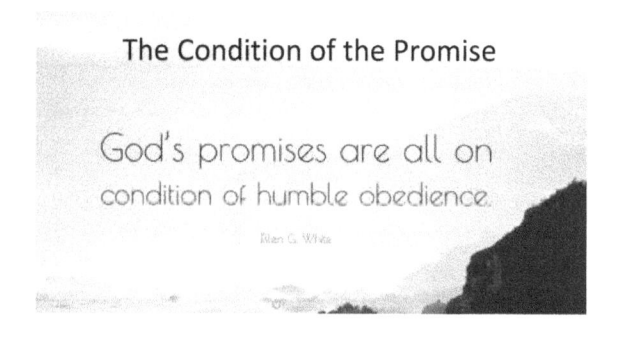

The Condition of the Promise

God's promises are all on condition of humble obedience.

Ellen G. White

Deborah Barnes
If My People

*A 12 Week Bible Study from the Devotional Book "Beyond the Sunday Sermon"*

## Key Messages about the Promise

The Confidence          The Completeness          The Condition

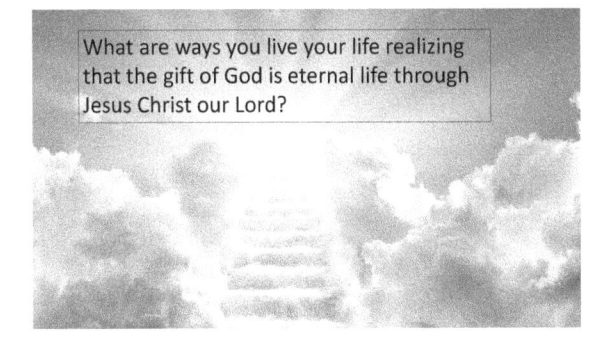

**JOURNAL DISCUSSION:**

BELIEVE THE PROMISE

What are ways you live your life realizing that the gift of God is eternal life through Jesus Christ our Lord?

What are ways you have changed your life according to God's commands?

55

*Ronald W. Holmes, Ph.D.*

**WHY IS THE FIRST COMMANDMENT SO IMPORTANT?**

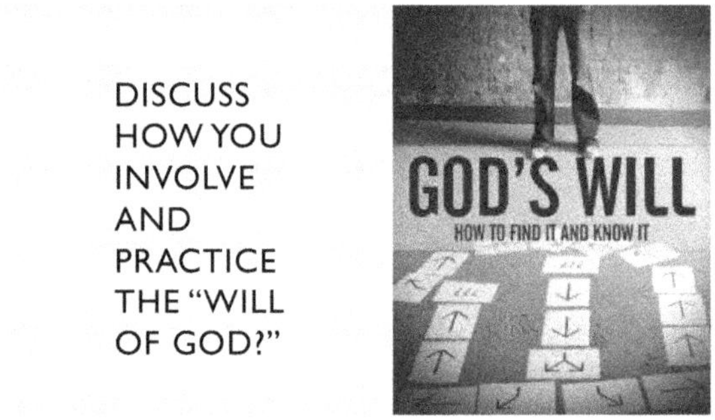

**DISCUSS HOW YOU INVOLVE AND PRACTICE THE "WILL OF GOD?"**

**SUMMARY**

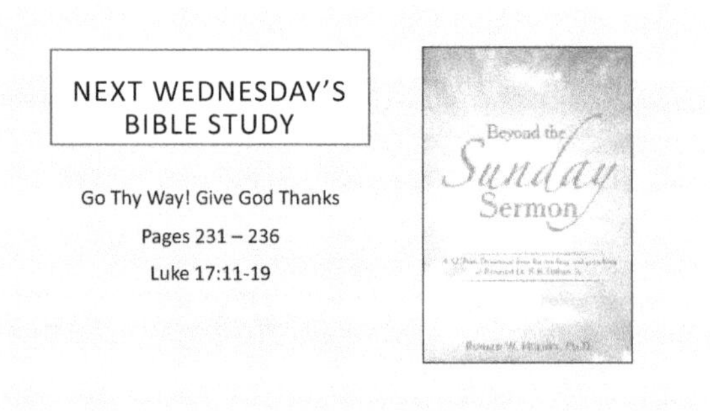

**NEXT WEDNESDAY'S BIBLE STUDY**

Go Thy Way! Give God Thanks
Pages 231 – 236
Luke 17:11-19

## WEEK 6

# Go Thy Way! Give God Thanks!

Good evening, Reverend Newbill, members, friends, and guest of First Timothy Baptist Church's Wednesday Night Bible Study. For such a time as this, if you are happy and you know it, clap your hands. If you are happy and you know it, stomp your feet. If you are blessed and you know it, praise the Lord on your feet or in your seat. First Timothy, we welcome you today in church and online for the lesson on Go Thy Way! Give God Thanks!

Former First Timothy Deacon R.B. Holmes Sr., my father in heaven, had the ability to gain good employment, maintain the employment, and refer a great number of his neighbors, friends, and family members for a job at his employer, the Jacksonville and Mayport Shipyards. After high school and while in graduate school, daddy got me a job at the Shipyard in downtown Jacksonville and Mayport. I respectfully thanked him and the employer for the job not only in words but also in my outstanding attendance, behavior, and performance on the job.

Each time we are blessed by God, we must graciously thank him for blessing us too; not only in our words but also in our unwavering praise, worship, support, and loyalty in the church. Using our teaching style for this bible study, we are going to (1) read an excerpt of the Sunday Sermon and Scripture from the book titled Beyond the Sunday Sermon; (2) discuss the four key points from the Sunday Sermon lesson; (3) provide concrete details to support the key points; and (4) summarize the lesson with scriptures and questions from the daily journal. At this time, Constance Holmes will come and read the excerpt of the lesson and scripture.

Thank you, Constance. Now, let's look closely at the four key points about the lepers. The lesson focuses on (1) their condition; (2) their cry; (3) their cure; and (4) their character.

## Key Point 1:

Jesus is passing through Samaria and Galilee and sees the condition of the 10 lepers (Luke 17:11-12). The lepers have the deadly and contagious skin disease of leprosy that causes the flesh to rotten and smell. The lepers are faced with a lonely and lasting disease. They are faced with a disease that does not care about a person's religion, nationality, race, sex, creed, position, rank, class, or status. It is a disease without limits; an equal opportunity destroyer, but Jesus is an equal opportunity restorer. What man meant for evil, like in the story of Mordecai that Rev. Newbill preached about on Sunday, God can turn it around and make it good (Genesis 50:20).

Just as we stood six feet social distancing away from people during the coronavirus, Jesus saw the lepers isolated in a certain village standing "far off" social distancing from each other (Luke 17: 12). While we had to wear a mask and isolate for approximately seven days once contracted with the coronavirus, the lepers had to wear a covering and shout unclean, unclean to keep the germs from spreading to other people (Leviticus 13:45).

During biblical times, there was no known cure for leprosy just like there was no known cure for the coronavirus at the beginning. People were ex-communicated from their family members, friends, church, schools, and social events. In the US, this probably was the worst of times. It was so bad that kids didn't know why they could not attend school and go outside and play with their friends; and families didn't know how to have family reunions without being impacted by the coronavirus; so I wrote a children's book to teach kids about COVID-19 and 10 ways to protect themselves and others from the disease. I also wrote a book to teach families how to plan an in person and virtual family reunion during a pandemic.

Therefore, when I think about the goodness of the Lord and how we got over the pandemic, I am very thankful, grateful, and appreciative. In fact, last week I was in a wheelchair under Mrs. Holmes' house care. This morning when I rose, I didn't have any doubt that I will be able to get off my couch and walk. I know the Lord will take care of me as illustrated in a song by the Mississippi Mass Choir. Take a listen to the song.

## Key Point 2:

Secondly, when our situation or condition in life gets the best of us, we must "cry out" to Jesus. We must "cry out" for his grace and mercy. Remember the story that Brother Terrence and the First Timothy Choir sang on Sunday about the disciples on a ship with Jesus who was asleep when a storm arose; and they woke him, and said "Master, carest thou not that we perish?" And Jesus "arose, and rebuked the wind, and said unto the sea, Peace, be still." And the wind ceased, and there was a great calm (Mark 4:38 & 39). Thus, the lepers heard Jesus was the Master of the winds and the waves. They knew Jesus could heal them; so when the ten lepers saw Jesus, "they lifted up their voices and said, Master have mercy on us" (Luke 17:13).

Until we "cry out" to Jesus (we have to cry sometimes), this country will never be healed. Remember, God said it in 2 Chronicles 7:14, "If my people, which are called by my name, shall humble themselves, and pray, and seek my face, and turn from their wicked ways; then will I hear from heaven, and will forgive their sin, and will heal their land."

## Key Point 3:

Thirdly, the Lord gave Moses' instructions on how to deal with the deadly disease of leprosy as cited in Leviticus 13: 1-2. When the Lord saw the lepers, he gave them instructions to see the priest (Luke 17: 14). Just like we had to show proof or test negative for being healed from COVID-19, the Lord used the priest to show proof or verify that the lepers were healed from leprosy before going back to their families and communities. Today, we even check your temperature before you enter church, doctor's offices, and other places for precautionary reasons.

Leprosy like sin has no human cure. What can wash away my sins? What can make me whole again? Nothing but the blood of Jesus. No amount of silver and gold; property and land; cash and class; clique and clout; prestige and power; prosperity and equity; media press and success will be enough to cure the sins in our life. Nothing but the blood of Jesus. Thus, we can't let anything keep us from confessing our sins. The bible teaches us in 1 John 1: 9: "If we confess our sins, he is faithful and just to forgive us our sins, and to cleanse us from all unrighteousness." Therefore, we must be steadfast in praising, worshiping, serving, and thanking the Lord for his grace and mercy.

## Key Point 4:

Fourth, many times we get jobs and do not thank the employer and person who helped us get the job; so I wrote a Business Communications book to teach high school and college students how to prepare for employment and thank people who referred and hired them for the job. To make my point, I would like to tell a story. Can I tell a story about when I worked at the Shipyard in Mayport, Florida.

In 1986, I was in graduate school and had a two month break before the next semester started. Through my daddy's reference, I was hired as a boiler maker. I wanted to make my daddy and employer proud of my work. As a graduate student, my co-workers did not think I would perform one of the toughest jobs down in the belly of the ship; but I persevered and did the heavy lifting. I worked side by side with a welder in extremely hot conditions pulling the old boiler tubes from the boiler room of the ship once he cut them. Each day, I reached the "dirty pay" requirement without any fuss, because my clothes were covered with dust. I worked so hard that the word traveled across the base that there was a college student hustling diligently to get the ship ready for the sea; so the head man of the shipyard wearing a "white hat" came to visit me. He yelled down to the belly of the ship, boiler maker! boiler maker! I replied, "Yes sir!" He said, "How much over time do you have?" I replied,

"None sir." He said, "Boiler maker from this day on, you can work as many overtime hours as you want." I replied, "Yes sir!"

When I returned to college, the ship returned to the sea and bombed the enemy. My daddy called me and said, "Son, I saw your supervisor; and the supervisor said, that man works! He can work for me anytime, any day, or any place." That day, family, I knew I had made my daddy and employer proud. In addition to words, this was the way I thanked them for the job.

On a similar note, many times the Lord blesses us, and we do not thank him for the blessing. Consider the Lepers' character. All of them got healed (right?); but only one showed his character by graciously thanking and glorifying the Lord for healing him (Luke 17: 15-16). The other nine demonstrated their character by being ungracious, unthankful, and unappreciative. Jesus acknowledged that there were ten lepers he healed but recognized that the other nine were missing in action, so to speak (Luke 17:17); and the only leper that returned to praise him was a stranger (Luke 17:18); so Jesus spoke to the man that thanked him and said, "Arise and go thy way, thy faith hath made thee whole" (Luke 17: 19).

First Timothy, do you know how to receive every blessing from the Lord? Yes! In this biblical story, Jesus healed the nine lepers, but they did not know how to receive the blessing. As believers, the Bible teaches us in Psalm 34:1 that we must "bless the Lord at all times" whether we are rich or poor; fortunate or unfortunate; healthy or sick; strong or weak; joyful or remorseful; patient or impatient; and free or isolated from COVID-19. "For God so loved the world, that he gave his only begotten Son, that whosoever believeth in Him should not perish, but have everlasting life" (John 3:16). We must grow strong in our faith, and ask the Lord, if we are ungracious, unthankful, and unappreciative like the nine lepers, to teach us how to receive every blessing as illustrated in a song by Brian Courtney Wilson. Take a listen to the song.

In summary, First Timothy, this lesson focused on the story of the 10 lepers regarding their condition, cry, cure, and character. If we did not get anything from the lesson, we must remember to give God thanks for all he is doing in our lives. He woke us this morning; and started us on our way. He enabled us to attend bible study today. Amen. At this time, let's reflect on some of the daily journal questions about leprosy from the book, "Beyond the Sunday Sermon." Constance will lead the discussion.

We are now at the end of the bible study. We hope you have gained something from this bible study. We look forward to your participation in next Wednesday's lesson titled Be Great! Serve! (Pages 237 - 242) from the book *"Beyond the Sunday Sermon."* The scripture is: St. Mark 9: 33 - 37. If you would like to read some summaries about the bible study at First Timothy, go to the website of The Holmes Education Post. You will find the summaries in the religion section of the website.

Now, we will have closing remarks from Reverend Newbill.

*Ronald W. Holmes, Ph.D.*

# WEEK 6: Outline of Service

First Timothy Wednesday Night Bible Study
October 11, 2023
7:00PM – 8:00PM

Message: Go Thy Way! Give God Thanks!
from the book *"Beyond the Sunday Sermon"* (Pages 231 - 236)
Scripture: St. Luke 17:11-19 KJV

| Time | What | By Whom | Music to play or Visual to Display |
|---|---|---|---|
| 6:53PM – 7:00PM | Song/video: I'll Just Say Yes by Brian Courtney Wilson (7:01) | Media Ministry to play song/video | • Play song/music – I'll Just Say Yes |
| 7:00PM -7:03PM | Prayer and Intro of Wednesday Night Bible Study | Rev. Newbill or Minister Melton | • Show Slide 1 – Wednesday Night Bible Study |
| 7:03PM – 7:05PM | Intro & Teaching Method | Dr. Ronald Holmes | • Show Slide 2– Welcome/Ronald |
| 7:05PM – 7:10PM | Reading the Excerpt of Sunday Sermon & Scripture | Constance Holmes | • Slide 3 – Jesus Heals the Lepers |
| 7:10PM – 7:18PM | • Four Key Points from the Message<br>• Supporting Details from the Message | Dr. Ronald Holmes | • Slide 4,5,6 - Key Messages |
| 7:18PM –7:23PM | Song/Video:<br>• This Morning When I Rose – (Cut off at 5:35) Mississippi Mass Choir | Media Ministry to play music video | • Slide 7 to show until Music Video Starts Playing<br>• Play music video/song –This Morning When I Rose |
| 7:23PM –7:28PM | • Continue with Key Point Message 2,3,4 | Dr. Ronald Holmes | • Slide 8,9,10,11,12 - Key Messages 2,3 &4 |
| 7:28PM –7:36PM | • Song/Video: Every Blessing (8:29) Brian Courtney Wilson | Media Ministry to play music video | • Slide 13 to show until Music Video starts<br>• Play music video/song –Every Blessing |

*A 12 Week Bible Study from the Devotional Book "Beyond the Sunday Sermon"*

| 7:36PM – 7:37PM | • Summarize key points | Dr. Ronald Holmes | • Slide 14 – Summary of Key Points |
|---|---|---|---|
| 7:37PM – 7:55PM | Facilitated discussion of Daily Journal from the Book-Pages 234-236 | Constance Holmes | • Slides 15 -18- as each is being discussed |
| 7:55PM – 7:56 | Summary of Bible Study | Dr. Ronald Holmes | • Slide 19 |
| 7:56PM – 8:00PM | Closing Comments & Prayer | Reverend Newbill or Minister Melton | • Continue with Slide 19 |

- I'll Just Say Yes- https://www.youtube.com/watch?v=mZ_sMqDYWj8
- This Morning When I Rose – https://youtu.be/AXTk46IfDTg?si=zSYNbZemy938RD0v
- Every Blessing - https://youtu.be/5GOxF0JLOBo?si=HGSnXwEaXhnBNlpU

Ronald W. Holmes, Ph.D.

# WEEK 6: Visual Slides

Go Thy Way!
Give God Thanks!

Key Messages about the Lepers

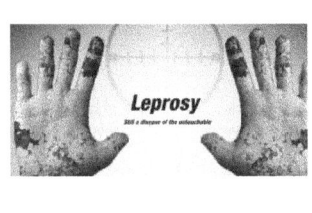

Their Condition | Their Cry | Their Cure | Their Character

1. Their Condition

**Leprosy**
Still a disease of the untouchable

**Jacob's Dream!**
A Children's Guide to Understanding the Coronavirus (COVID-19)
Ronald W. Holmes, Ph.D.

**A Roadmap for Planning**
an in person, and virtual family reunion during a pandemic
Ronald W. Holmes, Ph.D.

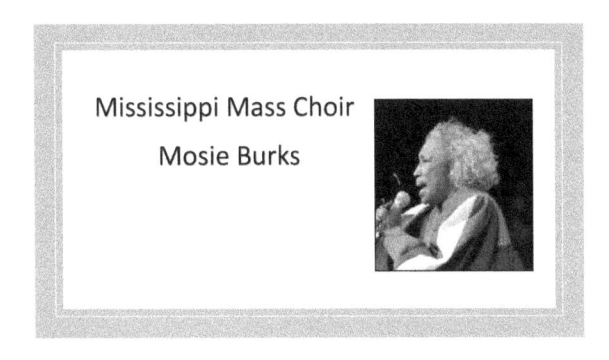

*A 12 Week Bible Study from the Devotional Book "Beyond the Sunday Sermon"*

Mississippi Mass Choir

Mosie Burks

2. Their Cry

3. Their Cure

*Ronald W. Holmes, Ph.D.*

## Their Character

A Business Communications & Grammar Book for High School and College Students

Ronald W. Holmes, Ph.D.

THIS IS MY STORY.

Brian Courtney Wilson
Every Blessing

*A 12 Week Bible Study from the Devotional Book "Beyond the Sunday Sermon"*

## In Summary…..

| Their Condition | Their Cry | Their Cure | Their Character |

**JOURNAL DISCUSSION:**

**GO THY WAY! GIVE GOD THANKS!**

### Question #1

Why is the story about the ten lepers so important? What messages do you get from the story to apply to your life today?

### Question #2

Discuss examples of your obeying the Lord and the benefits you received thereafter.

## Question #3

Only one leper returned to praise and glorify God. What was the significance of the one? Why did God ask about the other nine lepers? How do you apply this message to your life?

Next Wednesday's Bible Study

Be Great! Serve!
Pages 237–242
St.Mark 9:33-37

## WEEK 7

# Be Great! Serve!

The greatest commandment of God is to love him with all your heart, soul, and mind (Matthew 22 – 36 – 38).

Good evening, Reverend Newbill, Reverend Dr. & Mrs. R.B. Holmes, Jr., members, friends, and other guest of First Timothy Baptist Church's Wednesday Night Bible Study. We welcome you this evening in church and online for the lesson on Be Great! Serve!

In this world, there are ongoing discussions about who is the greatest athlete of all time. Many sports analysts claim that gymnast Simone Biles; tennis player Serena Williams; and golf player Jack Nicholas are the greatest in their respective sports. While analysts' opinions vary over time, we will highlight what greatness look like from a biblical perspective.

Using our teaching style for this bible study, we are going to (1) read an excerpt of the Sunday Sermon and Scripture from the book titled Beyond the Sunday Sermon; (2) discuss the three key points from the Sunday Sermon lesson; (3) provide concrete details to support the key points; and (4) summarize the lesson with scriptures and questions from the daily

journal. At this time, Constance Holmes will come and read the excerpt of the lesson and scripture.

Thank you, Constance. Now, let's look closely at the three key points about greatness from a biblical perspective. The lesson focuses on how to (1) be greater (2) do greater; and (3) get greater through Jesus Christ.

## Key Point 1:

This lesson teaches us to resist the temptation for self-promotion if we are going to be a greater race, people, boss, employer, school, church, and country. Self-promotion is attempting to present yourself to others as an accomplished, capable, smart, and skilled person. It is presenting yourself as though you are all of this and that, so to speak. The temptation of self-promotion can be done through social media outlets such as Facebook which has three billion users worldwide. The temptation of self-promotion can also be done through cellular phones where over 92 million selfies are snapped every day in the world. People enjoy looking at themselves and interacting on social media platforms for self-gratification, appreciation, and motivation.

In our text, the disciples had a serious argument about who was the greatest (Mark 9:33 -34). The disciples' minds were on human concerns rather than the concerns of Jesus even during the time he was discussing his death and burial with them (Mark 8: 31 – 33). The bible says in Mark 9: 17 -18, the disciples were approached by a man who brought his very sick son to them to cast out a demon; but they were unable to heal the child. The father of the child "cried out" to Jesus and said with tears in his eyes, "Lord, I believe, help thou mine unbelief" (Mark 9: 24); and Jesus the High Priest healed the child at the man's request as recorded in Mark 9: 25 – 27. The disciples wanted to know from Jesus why they could not heal the child (Mark 9:28); and Jesus answered to them that they lacked prayer and fasting to heal the child as recorded in Mark 9: 29. Jesus, acknowledged and assessed that the disciples were more concerned about their title than service in the kingdom; so Jesus explained to them what their status, position, or title will be in the in kingdom as recorded in Luke 22: 24 - 30.

We have learned through our reading the bible and worshiping in church that a testimony is more important than a title. For example, Haman had a title, but Mordecai had a testimony. Goliath had a title, but David had a testimony. Pharoah had a title, but Mosses had a testimony. The Syrians had a title, but the four Lepers had a testimony. Nebuchadnezzar had a title, but Shadrack, Meshack, and Abednego had a testimony. Pilate had a title, but Jesus, the Messiah, the Savior, the Vine, the High Priest, the Prince of Peace, the Lilly of the Valley, the Bright and Morning Star, the Kings of Kings, and Lord of Lords had a testimony. Do I have a witness? We have also learned from T.V., a Canadian Funeral Home Corporation had a title, but Jeremiah O'Keefe, represented by Attorney Willie Gary, had a testimony.

The word of God teaches us we must resist self-promotion as written in Philippians 2: 3. In essence, don't just think about yourselves or do anything for selfish purposes; but with humility think of other people as more important than yourselves. We must become Christ-centered, people centered rather than self-centered. On this note, I am reminded of a story of a self-centered, selfish, egotistical, and conceited boss. This story was discovered when I interviewed an employee for my book on *Eradicating Workplace Bullying: A Guide for Every Organization.* Can I tell the story about this selfish boss better known as a gatekeeper bully who was consumed or obsessed with being in control? Take a listen to the story.

Marilyn Madison, a fake name I used for confidentiality purposes, was a new assistant principal at a school where student discipline and academic performance were a major challenge for school officials. Madison assessed the needs of the students and started implementing ideas to address their concerns. After Madison's hiring, a new principal whose characteristics resembled that of a selfish boss or gatekeeper bully was brought to the school to eliminate the discipline and academic problems. The principal discredited all the ideas and input of Madison and ignored the concerns of the students at the school. It was not until a major catastrophe occurred at the school and a parent advisory member publicly said, "The best way to deal with the problem at the school is to adopt the ideas of Madison." Reluctantly, the principal adopted the ideas of Madison and, subsequently, this problem at the school and others were resolved. This gave Madison credibility among stakeholders such as students, teachers, staff, and parents. However, the principal being a selfish boss refused to acknowledge the many contributions that Madison rendered to the school, questioned her work performance, and publicly referenced Madison's ideas as his own. The principal was more concerned about his needs, status, title, and credibility instead of Madison and other stakeholders at the school. The principal eventually left the school and tried to stop Madison from advancing in her profession.

As believers, we must remember that "weeping may endure for a night, but joy cometh in the morning" (Psalm 30:5). What man meant for evil, God can turn it around and make it good (Genesis 50: 20). Madison was promoted to a higher position after her selfish boss left the school. This is an example of how God will protect you from danger seen or unseen.

Sometimes God keeps you from getting certain positions and staying in certain positions because they are a mismatch to your faith. This is an example of what God has for me is for me. I know without a doubt; He will bring me out as illustrated in a song by the Miami Mass Choir. Take a listen to the song.

## Key Point 2:

Secondly, service is better than status and title in God's kingdom. The selfish boss was more concerned about his status than the people in the school. He had an "I" "I" "I" and "Me" "Me" "Me" mentality. He was insecure of himself. By being a servant to all, we can do greater things in a school, industry, organization, and church (Mark 9:35). Take the Alpha Phi Alpha Fraternity, Incorporated, for example. In 1906, this fraternity was established at an Ivy League school named Cornell University. Our Fraternity's motto of first of all, servants of all, we shall transcend all embodies our history as the first intercollegiate Fraternity founded by African American men.

Our mission is to provide service to our community. Some great men have become members of this prestigious fraternity such as Reverend Dr. Martin Luther King Jr., Supreme Court Justice Thurgood Marshall, Mayor Maynard Jackson, and Reverend Dr. R.B. Holmes, Jr. who is present with us today.

Our beloved Alpha brother, Dr. King, made it very clear that "Everybody can be great because everybody can serve. You don't have to have a college degree to serve. You only need a heart full of grace; a soul generated by love" (Goodreads.com). Thus, be of good faith and servant to all. "For God resisteth the proud, and giveth grace to the humble" (1 Peter 5:5).

Humble yourselves therefore under the mighty hand of God, that he may exalt you in due time" (1 Peter 5:6). Keep your eyes on Jesus who is the "author and finisher of our faith" (Hebrews 12: 2).

## Key Point 3:

Thirdly, Jesus is the answer for the world today. There is no other; Jesus is the way. Jesus loves the little children. He says the child is the example or epitome of being great; Jesus took a child, and set him in the midst of the disciples (Mark 9: 36; and Matthew 18: 2). He said to them "except ye be converted and become like little children; you will never enter the kingdom of heaven" (Matthew 18: 3).

Therefore, the best way to get greater in our life is through our Lord and Savior Jesus Christ. "Greater is he that is in you than he that is in the world" (1 John 4:4). With that said, I would like to share with you the words of two songs that highlight how to get greater through Christ. The words to the first song, a favorite of my father reads: A charge to keep I have, a God to glorify, a never-dying soul to save, and fit it for the sky. To serve the present age, my calling to fulfill; O may it all my powers engage, to do my Master's will! The words to the second song reads: If I can help somebody, as I travel along. If I can help somebody, with a word or song. If I can help somebody, from doing wrong. No, my living shall not be in vain.

By serving others, we serve not only Jesus but also His father (Mark 9:37). Serving others will bring approval of the Lord and His father. Thus, true greatness is measured by service to all humankind. We learn true greatness from and through Jesus. He is the Great I am who died for our salvation; so it is more blessed to give than to receive" (Acts 20:35). In fact, the more you give, the more God gives to you; so just keep on giving because it's really true. That you can't beat God's giving no matter how you try. For meditation, take a listen to a song about giving.

In summary, First Timothy, this lesson focused on what true greatness looks like from a biblical perspective. It emphasized how to be greater, do greater, and get greater through Jesus Christ. Just like the brothers of Alpha Phi Alpha, let's be of service to our community. Let's be great and serve! Amen.

At this time, let's reflect on some of the daily journal questions on "serve" from the book, "Beyond the Sunday Sermon." Constance will lead the discussion.

We are now at the end of Bible Study. We certainly hope you have gained something from this Bible Study. We look forward to your participation in next Wednesday's lesson titled The Gift of Jesus (Pages 243 - 248) from the book *"Beyond the Sunday Sermon."* The scripture is: Isaiah 9: 6. If you would like to read some news articles about the bible study at First Timothy, go to the website of The Holmes Education Post. You will find the articles in the religion section of the website.

Now, we will have closing remarks from Reverend Newbill.

Ronald W. Holmes, Ph.D.

# WEEK 7: Outline of Service

Outline of Service<br>
First Timothy Wednesday Night Bible Study<br>
October 18, 2023<br>
7:00PM – 8:00PM

Message: Be Great! Serve!
from the book *"Beyond the Sunday Sermon"* (Pages 237 - 242)
Scripture: St. Mark 9:33-37 KJV

| Time | What | By Whom | Music to play or Visual to Display |
|---|---|---|---|
| 6:53PM – 7:00PM | Song/video: I'll Just Say Yes by Brian Courtney Wilson (7:01) | Media Ministry to play song/video | • Play song/music – I'll Just Say Yes |
| 7:00PM -7:03PM | Prayer and Intro of Wednesday Night Bible Study | Rev. Newbill or Minister Melton | • Show Slide 1 – Wednesday Night Bible Study |
| 7:03PM – 7:05PM | Intro & Teaching Method | Dr. Ronald Holmes | • Show Slide 1&2– Welcome/Ronald |
| 7:05PM – 7:10PM | Reading the Excerpt of Sunday Sermon & Scripture | Constance Holmes | • Slide 3 – Be Great! Serve! |
| 7:10PM – 7:18PM | • Three Key Points from the Message<br>• Supporting Details from the Message | Dr. Ronald Holmes | • Slide 4,5,6, - Key Messages |
| 7:18PM –7:23PM | Song/Video:<br>• It Is For Me – (5:22) Miami Mass Choir | Media Ministry to play music video | • Slide 7 to show until Music Video Starts Playing<br>• Play music video/song –It Is For Me |
| 7:23PM –7:28PM | • Continue with Key Messages 2&3 | Dr. Ronald Holmes | • Slide 8,9,10 - Key Messages 2&3 |
| 7:28PM –7:36PM | • Song/Video: You Can't Beat God Giving (4:07) Billy Preston | Media Ministry to play music video | • Slide 11 to show until Music Video starts<br>• Play music video/song –You Can't Beat God Giving |

| 7:36PM – 7:37PM | • Summarize Key Points | Dr. Ronald Holmes | • Slide 12 – Summary of Key Points |
|---|---|---|---|
| 7:37PM – 7:55PM | Facilitated discussion of Daily Journal from the Book-Pages 240 - 242 | Constance Holmes | • Slides 13 -16 - as each question is being discussed |
| 7:55PM – 7:56 | Summary of Bible Study | Dr. Ronald Holmes | • Slide 17 & 18 |
| 7:56PM – 8:00PM | Closing Comments & Prayer | Reverend Newbill or Minister Melton | • Continue with Slide 19 |

- I'll Just Say Yes- https://www.youtube.com/watch?v=mZ_sMqDYWj8
- It is For Me – https://youtu.be/-CmSN52DgtQ?si=STtmdcXbHqrLOYhk
- You Can't Beat God Giving - https://youtu.be/_tqM5GJ-tg0?si=CV_u3_oyEUYe7VbI

# WEEK 7: Visual Slides

### Key Messages about Greatness

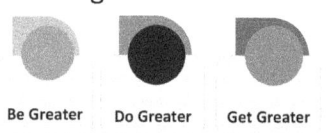

Be Greater   Do Greater   Get Greater

**1. Be Greater: Resist Self Promotion**

A Story: The Selfish Boss

*ERADICATING WORKPLACE BULLYING*

*A 12 Week Bible Study from the Devotional Book "Beyond the Sunday Sermon"*

Miami Mass Choir – It Is For Me

2.
Do Greater: Service is Better than Status

IF ANYONE WANTS TO BE *First*, HE SHALL BE LAST OF ALL AND SERVANT OF ALL.

Great Alpha Phi Alpha Servant Leaders

And said, Verily I say unto you, Except ye be converted, and become as little children, ye shall not enter into the kingdom of heaven. Matthew 18:3

3. Get Greater through Jesus Christ

Ronald W. Holmes, Ph.D.

**Billy Preston**
**You Can't Beat God Giving**

## Key Messages about Greatness

- Be Greater
- Do Greater
- Get Greater

**JOURNAL DISCUSSION:**

**BE GREAT! SERVE!**

**LET YOUR light SHINE**

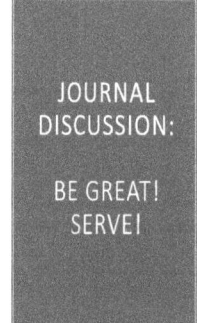

Question #1

Discuss examples of how you let your light shine before men and women so they could see your good work and glorify God.

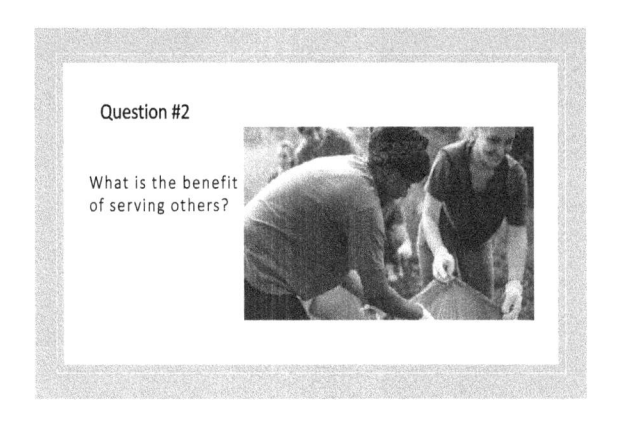

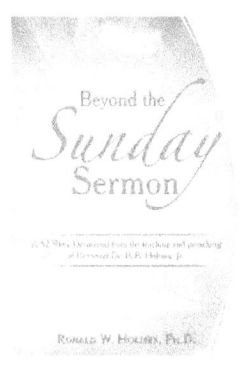

*A 12 Week Bible Study from the Devotional Book "Beyond the Sunday Sermon"*

**Question #2**

What is the benefit of serving others?

**Question #3**

Why is it bad to serve two masters?

## Next Wednesday's Bible Study

**The Gift of Jesus**
Pages 243 - 248
Isaiah 9:6

*Ronald W. Holmes, Ph.D.*

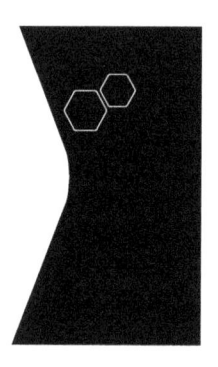

WEEK 8

# The Gift of Jesus

Good evening, Reverend Newbill, members, friends, and guests of First Timothy Baptist Church's Wednesday Night Bible Study. We welcome you today in church and online for the lesson on The Gift of Jesus!

When I was a child, I spoke, understood, and thought like a child as recorded in 1 Corinthians 13: 11. Childish things such as toys, clothes, and allowances that I wished for on my birthday were gifts for the special occasion. The excitement of my birthday was second to none. Although I was happy about the gifts for my birthday, this lesson will focus on the gift of Jesus.

Using our teaching style for this bible study, we are going to (1) read an excerpt of the Sunday Sermon and Scripture from the book titled *"Beyond the Sunday Sermon;"* (2) discuss the three key points from the Sunday Sermon lesson; (3) provide concrete details to support the key points; and (4) summarize the lesson with scriptures and questions from the daily journal.

Constance Holmes, my wife, is not here with us today. She is in Lancaster, South Carolina giving healthcare, loving care, and family care to her

88-year-old brother, Dr. James Coleman. In her absence, Sister Lorraine Rhodes, will come and read the excerpt of the lesson and scripture.

Thank you, Sister Rhodes. Now, let's look closely at the three key points for today's lesson. The lesson focuses on (1) the birth of Jesus (2) the boldness of Jesus; and (3) the blessings of Jesus.

## Key Point 1:

"For God so loved the world that he gave his only begotten son, that whosoever believeth in him should not perish, but have everlasting life" (John 3: 16). With that said, we must confess Jesus Christ as our Lord and Savior to be saved, be delivered from sin, and have eternal life.

As a believer, I will not try to convince you that Jesus was born on December 25; but I know he was born. I will not engage in an intellectual discussion with you about the date, time, or season of Jesus' birth; I just know he was born and one day he was born in me.

As believers, First Timothy, we all know that he was born in a manger in Bethlehem (Luke 2: 7). We know that "the angels said unto them, fear not, behold, I bring you good tidings (meaning good news) of great joy, which shall be to all people" (Luke 2:10). "For unto you is born this day a Saviour which is Christ the Lord" (Luke 2:11). "And this shall be a sign unto you; ye shall find the babe wrapped in swaddling clothes lying in a manger (Luke 2:12).

The gift of Jesus came to earth over two thousand years ago. Jesus was perfectly wrapped by the power of the Holy Ghost. He was delivered not by Amazon, UPS, or FedEx; but by a virgin woman named Mary. The name that came on the package of the gift was "whosoever believeth in him should not perish, but have everlasting life (John 3: 16).

As believers, we also know before Jesus' birth, it was spoken by the Lord through a prophet that "a virgin shall be with child, and shall bring forth a son, and they shall call his name Emmanuel, which being interpreted is, God with us" (Matthew 1:22 – 23).

God moves in mysterious ways. His wonders to perform. "For unto us a son is given; and his name shall be called Wonderful, Counsellor, The mighty God, The everlasting Father, and the Prince of Peace" (Isaiah 9:6). Who is "us?" Does the word "us" mean everyone? No! Isaiah is speaking only to the believers who accept Jesus as Lord and Savior as recorded in John 1:12: It reads, "But as many as received him, to them gave he power to become the sons of God even, to them that believe on his name." Are you a part of the "us" generation? As a gift, God has given to "us" his son. We must confess Jesus Christ as our Lord and Savior to be saved, be delivered from sin, and have eternal life.

Glory to the Newborn King. Let us give every praise to our God. He is Alpha and Omega, the bread of Life, the Redeemer, the Living Stone, and the Lamb of God. Glory to the Newborn King. Through Jesus, "I know that I can make it. I know I can stand. No matter what may come my way. My life is in his hands" as sang by Kirk Franklin. "Jesus, Jesus, oh, what a wonderful child. Jesus, Jesus so holy, meek, and mild. We listen to the angels sing, Glory to the Newborn King." Now, take a listen to this song, "Glory to the Newborn King" by the Angelic Gospel Singers.

## Key Point 2:

Secondly, we must get right with Jesus because this world will come to an end. Realizing we are faced with the troubles of the world (war, crime, inflation, pollution, infection, corruption, etc.), the good news is that one of these days, the government shall be upon Jesus' shoulder as recorded in Isaiah 9: 6. This is the boldness of Jesus as declared by Prophet Isaiah 3,000 years ago of the foreseeable future.

Let me park there about Jesus' boldness and tell you about my boldness when I was a nineth grader. Can I tell you the story? Ok! I boldly told my gym coach, Eddie, just one day in advance that I was going to outrun all the runners on his cross-country team. While we were sitting on the bleachers after dressing out from gym, the gym coach said, in a sarcastic way, all you guys can do is run fast. I said, "Coach, I will come out for cross country and outrun all your runners." I committed to my bold statement; and as we traveled to a big cross country meet out-of-town, I asked a senior who was the fastest runner on the team, to let me sit in the front seat since I had long legs. The senior runner responded no; then he said, "If you beat me, you can have the seat on our trip back home." The boldness of me beat him and everybody else on the team. When it was time to get my seat, the senior runner said no; however, the coach interrupted the conversation and said, "I heard the conversation; give it to him;" and I rode comfortably thereafter.

Now getting back to the text. The government shall be upon Jesus' shoulder as recorded in Isaiah 9:6. While I boldly gave the coach only one day in advance about what I was going to do, Jesus has given us (through Prophet Isaiah) 3,000 years in advance about what he is going to do upon his return to earth. There will be a new heaven and earth.

The former things will pass away. If I am saved and accept Jesus as my Lord and Savior, I don't have to fear about the government in the United States and abroad.

The government is going to be in the full jurisdiction of Jesus. According to Zechariah 14:9, "the Lord shall be king over all the earth: in that day shall there be one Lord, and his name one." All cities, countries and their governments will be devasted, destroyed, or annihilated. God shall "set up a kingdom, which shall never be destroyed: and the kingdom shall not be left to other people, but it shall break in pieces and consume all these kingdoms, and it shall stand forever (Daniel 2:44).

Jesus our Lord and Savior; the baby in a manger; now King of Kings and Lord of Lords. There is nobody like him. Jesus has all power in his hand. He loves us; he saves us. He endured the cross, and conquered death. He was born into sin so we could live again. He is the Precious Lamb of God. Now, let's meditate on this song, Precious Lamb of God, by Kirk Franklin!

## Key Point 3:

Thirdly, in this world, we will face trials and tribulations; and if we are not careful, these tribulations could get the best of our mental health. We must remember to rely on Jesus who is "the author and finisher of our faith" (Hebrews 12: 2). He is the answer for the world today, there is no other, Jesus is the way.

Jesus is full of wonder. Remember from bible study, he enabled blind Bartimaeus to see. Remember, he turned water into wine at a wedding. Remember, he healed a woman in the crowd with an issue of blood.

Remember, he cleansed 10 men with leprosy. Remember, he calmed a storm on a sea. Remember, he healed a boy with an unclean spirit. Jesus is the answer for the world today, yesterday, and tomorrow. He is omnipresent, omnipotent, universal, everywhere, all-powerful, supreme, and preeminent. In fact, as I said earlier, "His name shall be called Wonderful, Counsellor, the Mighty God, the Everlasting Father, and the Prince of Peace (Isaiah 9:6).

Let me clarify why his name shall be called as mentioned. Jesus was full of wonder at his birth. He was born of a virgin. He was announced by angels (Luke 2: 10-11). He was feared by demons. He was surrounded by shepherds (Luke 2: 8). He was provided gifts of gold, frankincense, and murr from kings (Matthew 2: 11). His birth was full of wonder. He is wonderful in his power to wake us early in the morning and start us on our way. That's a blessing!

Jesus is a Counselor because we have somebody we can talk to when we need comfort. He has "all" the answers to your questions. That's a blessing! He is the Mighty God because we have somebody with all power in his hand. He has more power than cancer, leprosy, COVID, the army, Navy, Airforce, Marines, Coast Guard, and National Guard. That's a blessing! He is "the way, truth, and the life" (John 14: 6). That's a blessing! If we lack wisdom, we can go to Jesus (James 1: 5). That's a blessing! "We can obtain mercy and find grace" from Jesus "in time of need" (Hebrews 4: 16) That's a blessing!

He is the Everlasting Father because we have somebody that death could not kill. Somebody who will be a father for us when we are fatherless. That's a blessing! Jesus is the Prince of Peace. He was anointed by God to save us from our sin and offers us eternal life. That's a blessing! In fact, that's the Gift of Jesus!

Therefore, the critical questions to be asked are: Do you know him? Have you tried him? Are you a witness for Jesus? Have you been strengthened spiritually since you gave him your life? Has he given you peace when facing difficult situations? Is he a mother or father for you during troubling times?

If he is, then you don't have to get depressed or stressed too long about bad news when you have the good news about Jesus. He is more than you need in this toxic world. He is wonderful. He is full of wonder.

On that note, there was a gospel song recorded in the 90's called, *"Jesus, What A Wonder You Are."* You are so gentle, so pure, and so kind. You shine, like a morning star. Jesus! what a wonder you are. For meditation and inspiration, take a listen to a song by Juanita Bynum her version of Jesus! What a wonder you are.

In summary, First Timothy, this lesson focused on the birth of Jesus, the boldness of Jesus, and the blessings of Jesus. We don't have to look for answers to our questions. We look to Jesus. He saves us from our sin and offers us eternal life. That's the gift of Jesus; so I leave you with three questions: (1) Have you opened your gift from Jesus? (2) Have you used your gift from Jesus? (3) Have you thanked Jesus for the gift? Amen.

At this time, let's reflect on some of the daily journal questions on "Birth" from the book, "Beyond the Sunday Sermon." Sister Lorraine Rhodes will lead the discussion.

*Ronald W. Holmes, Ph.D.*

We are now at the end of the bible study. We certainly hope you have gained something from this bible study. We look forward to your participation in next Wednesday's lesson titled The Promise of the Passover (Pages 249 - 254) from the book *"Beyond the Sunday Sermon."* The scripture is: Exodus 12:13, 21 – 31). If you would like to read some news articles about the bible study at First Timothy, go to the website of The Holmes Education Post. You will find the articles in the religion section of the website.

Now, we will have closing remarks from Reverend Newbill.

*A 12 Week Bible Study from the Devotional Book "Beyond the Sunday Sermon"*

# WEEK 8: Outline of Service

First Timothy Wednesday Night Bible Study
October 25, 2023
7:00PM – 8:00PM

Message: The Gift of Jesus
from the book *"Beyond the Sunday Sermon"* (Pages 243 - 248)
Scripture: Isaiah 9:6 KJV

| Time | What | By Whom | Music to play or Visual to Display |
|---|---|---|---|
| 6:53PM – 7:00PM | Song/video: I'll Just Say Yes by Brian Courtney Wilson (7:01) | Media Ministry to play song/video | • Play song/music – I'll Just Say Yes |
| 7:00PM -7:02PM | Prayer and Intro of Wednesday Night Bible Study | Rev. Newbill or Minister Milton | • Show Slide 1 – Wednesday Night Bible Study |
| 7:02PM – 7:05PM | Intro & Teaching Method | Dr. Ronald Holmes | • Show Slide 2– The Gift of Jesus |
| 7:05PM – 7:10PM | Reading the Excerpt of Sunday Sermon & Scripture | Loraine Rhodes | • Slide 2 – The Gift of Jesus |
| 7:10PM – 7:15PM | • Three Key Points from the Message<br>• Point #1 – The Birth of Jesus | Dr. Ronald Holmes | • Slide 3/4- Key Messages/Point #1-The Birth of Jesus |
| 7:15PM –7:18PM | Song/Video:<br>• Glory to the Newborn King – Angelic Gospel Singers (3:18) | Media Ministry to play music video | • Slide 5 to show until music video starts playing<br>• Play music video/ song –Glory to the Newborn King |
| 7:18PM –7:23PM | • Point #2 – The Boldness of Jesus | Dr. Ronald Holmes | • Slide 6 – Point# 2-The Boldness of Jesus |
| 7:23PM – 7:27PM | • Song/Video: The Precious Lamb of God – Kirk Franklin (4:08) | Media Ministry to play music video | • Play Slide 7 until music video starts<br>• Play music – The Precious Lamb of God |

| 7:27PM – 7:32 | • Point #3 -The Blessing of Jesus | Dr. Ronald Holmes | • Slide -8 – Point #3 The Blessing of Jesus |
|---|---|---|---|
| 7:32PM –7:38PM | • Song/Video: Jesus, What a Wonder You Are – Juanita Bynum (6:07) | Media Ministry to play music video | • Slide - 9 to show until music video starts<br>• Play music video/ song – Jesus, What a Wonder You Are |
| 7:38PM – 7:39PM | • Summarize Three Key Points | Dr. Ronald Holmes | • Slide 10 – Summary of Key Points |
| 7:39PM – 7:55PM | Facilitated discussion of Daily Journal from the Book-Pages 246 - 248 | Loraine Rhodes | • Slides 11 -14 - as each question is being discussed |
| 7:55PM – 7:56PM | Summary of Bible Study | Dr. Ronald Holmes | • Slide 15 & 16 |
| 7:56PM – 8:00PM | Closing Comments & Prayer | Reverend Newbill or Minister Milton | • Continue with Slide 17 |

- I'll Just Say Yes- https://www.youtube.com/watch?v=mZ_sMqDYWj8
- Glory to the King – https://youtu.be/MlvxmYs2noY?si=ZzxUGSYeenl1xHAj
- Precious Lamb of God - https://youtu.be/o2cWckjw2SU?si=-_cy7dnslZOscmDM
- Jesus, What a Wonder You Are - https://youtu.be/FVq4rkd-OSo?si=Ou6k0-GaNkfvQfjG

*A 12 Week Bible Study from the Devotional Book "Beyond the Sunday Sermon"*

# WEEK 8: Visual Slides

**WELCOME TO FIRST TIMOTHY** — KJV
Wednesday Night Bible Study

The Gift of Jesus

## Key Messages about the Gift of Jesus

- The Birth of Jesus
- The Boldness of Jesus
- The Blessings of Jesus

*Ronald W. Holmes, Ph.D.*

1. The Birth of Jesus

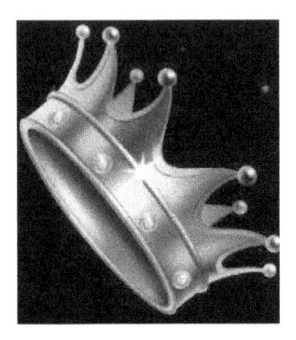

The Angelic Gospel Singers

Glory to the Newborn King

2. The Boldness of Jesus

Kirk Franklin

The Precious Lamb of God

*A 12 Week Bible Study from the Devotional Book "Beyond the Sunday Sermon"*

# 3. The Blessings of Jesus

## Juanita Bynum

Jesus, What A Wonder You Are

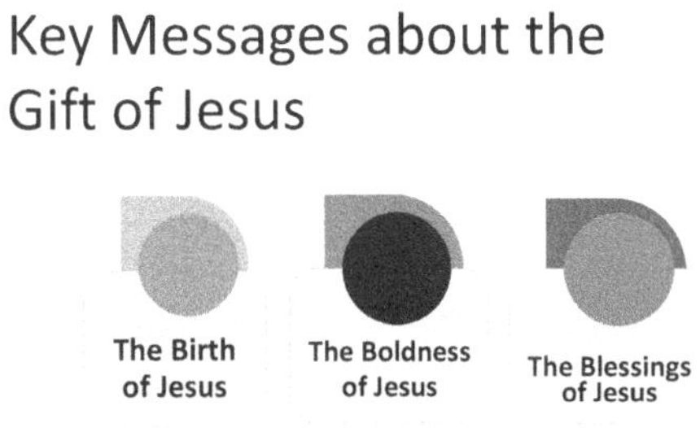

## Key Messages about the Gift of Jesus

- The Birth of Jesus
- The Boldness of Jesus
- The Blessings of Jesus

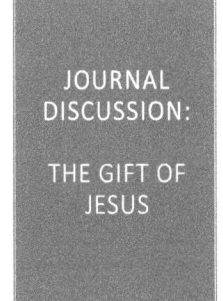

**JOURNAL DISCUSSION:**

**THE GIFT OF JESUS**

97

**Question #1**

What lesson is to be learned from John 3:16?

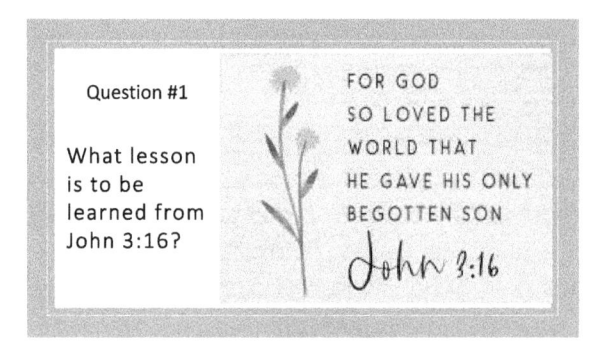

FOR GOD SO LOVED THE WORLD THAT HE GAVE HIS ONLY BEGOTTEN SON

John 3:16

**Question 2**

Why is it important to have a relationship with Jesus?

RELATIONSHIP WITH JESUS

**Question #3**

Discuss how the Lord has been a counselor to you.

WONDERFUL COUNSELOR mighty god EVERLASTING FATHER PRINCE OF PEACE - ISAIAH 9:6 -

## Next Wednesday's Bible Study

**The Promise of the Passover**
Pages 249 - 254
Exodus 12:13, 21-31

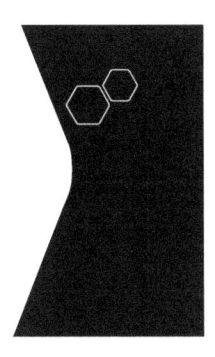

*A 12 Week Bible Study from the Devotional Book "Beyond the Sunday Sermon"*

## WEEK 9

# The Promise of the Passover

Let Everything that has Breath Praise the Lord. Good evening, Reverend Frederick Newbill, Reverend Dr. R.B. & Dr. Gloria Holmes, members, friends, and other guest of First Timothy Baptist Church's Wednesday Night Bible Study. We welcome you today in church and online for the lesson on The Promise of the Passover!

God has a purpose for our life just as he had a purpose for the Israelites. God promised he will never leave us nor forsake us (Hebrews 13:5). He said, "Occupy till I come" (Luke 19:13). We don't know the date or hour of Jesus' second coming to earth (Matthew 24: 36), but we know he promised to come "as a thief in the night" (1 Thessalonians 5: 2). We know that he promised that "whosoever shall call upon the name of the Lord shall be saved" (Romans 10:13). Considering the countless promises of the Lord, this lesson will focus on The Promise of the Passover.

Using our teaching style for this bible study, we are going to (1) read an excerpt of the Sunday Sermon and Scripture from the book titled *"Beyond the Sunday Sermon;"* (2) discuss the three key points from the Sunday Sermon lesson; (3) provide concrete details to support the key points; and (4) summarize the lesson with scriptures and questions from the daily journal. Constance Holmes will come and read the excerpt of the lesson and scripture.

Thank you, Constance. Now, let's look closely at the three key points for today's lesson. The lesson focuses on the life of the Israelites through (1) the preparation for the Passover (2) the purpose of the Passover; and (3) the power of the Passover.

## Key Point 1:

When we prepare for something such as school, church, and work, we make ready for the outing beforehand. When Constance and I moved to Atlanta, Georgia in the early 90's, I had to prepare her how to travel from home to work. I told her the exact streets and interstates to travel to eliminate any confusion for getting to work and coming home. However, my instructions did not go as planned. Can I tell you the story about this matter? Ok. I asked Constance to repeat to me the instructions on how she was going to get to work, and she mumbled the directions to me in an uncertain, unfamiliar, and unusual way; so I quickly stopped Constance from trying to explain her traveling route to me and drove her to work as a practice run.

When it was time for Constance to drive to work the next day, I asked her the same question about how she was going to travel; and I got the same reaction. At that moment, all I could visualize was an eighteen-wheeler running Constance off the road; so I took her to work to make sure she did not get lost or encounter an accident. I made sure she was prepared physically and mentality for her arrival to work.

Prior to the Lord's second coming, we must be prepared for his arrival to earth. We must get our house in order. This was the case for the Israelites who had to prepare for the Passover as instructed by God in Exodus 12: 21 – 22. God told Moses to prepare the Israelites for a great deliverance from bondage. They had to "put on the whole armor of God" so they could stand during this evil time (Ephesians 6: 11). The Israelites had been in captivity for over 400 years. The Lord said, I'm going to do a new thing (Isaiah 43: 19).

In doing so, the Lord instructed the Israelites to put the blood on the doorpost (Exodus 12: 22); He said, the blood will be your sign on the houses where you live. "Whenever I see the blood, I'll pass over you;" and no plague will destroy you when I strike the land of Egypt (Exodus 12: 13). Also, don't go outside the house until the next morning (Exodus 12: 22). In other words, don't go golfing, shopping, or dining. Stay inside, Israelites, until the next morning allowing sufficient time for the storm to pass over. You can't beat Pharoah with your army, but I can because I have all power in my hand. I created the heaven and the earth. I am the Great I am. I am King of Kings. I am Lord of Lords. I am Wonderful. I am a Counsellor. I am the Mighty God. I am the Everlasting Father. I am the Prince of Peace. I am anointed by God to save you from your sins and tribulations and offer you eternal life.

This is the preparation for the Passover which is one of the most powerful and supernatural events during biblical time. If we are going to defeat the Pharoah of today, we must listen to God, do what he tells us, and "put on the whole armor" of the Lord so we can stand during the evil time (Ephesians 6:11). If we are going to defeat the Pharoah of today, we must believe God is "the way, truth, and life" (John 14: 6). If we are going to defeat the Pharoah of today, we must believe God "is able to do exceedingly more than we ask" (Ephesians 3:20). We must believe. Do You Believe that God can make a way out of no way, open doors that are closed, hear our concerns, answer our prayers, restore our soul, fight our battles through different means, speak on our behalf, and never forsake us as illustrated in a song titled, I believe God, by Jekalyn Carr? Take a listen to the song.

## Key Point 2:

Secondly, when we have a purpose for something, it will provide how the situation, activity, or event is going to be done. The purpose of the Passover was to keep the Israelites alive while God was killing everything in the land of Egypt such as the first-born and first-born animals (Exodus 12: 29). The Passover provides an illustration of what God can do when he has had enough of our ignorance, arrogance, bigotry, selfishness, foolishness, stupidity, and captivity of his people. The Passover provides an illustration of the binding power of the covenant of the blood.

As recorded in Exodus 12:23, "For the Lord will pass through to smite the Egyptians; and when he seeth the blood upon the lintel, and on the two side posts, the Lord will pass over the door, and will not suffer the destroyer to come in unto your houses to smite you." Nothing, absolutely nothing in this world, can overtake you when you are covered by the blood of the Lamb. This is illustrated in Revelation 12:11. It reads, "they overcame him, by the blood of the Lamb, and by the word of their testimony; and they loved not their lives unto death." "So, how did the story end? I am glad you asked the question. The Lord broke the generational curse. He set the captives free. He commanded the Israelites to observe forever what happened to them and their children as a ritual; maintain the ritual when they enter the land he promised them; and be ready to respond to their children about the ritual when asked (Exodus 12: 24 – 26).

What did the Israelites do when the Lord set them free? Did they go back to business as usual as Pharoah did after the Lord sent nine plagues to Egypt to force him to release the Israelites (Exodus 7:14-11:10)? Did they go back to business as usual as the nine lepers did when the Lord cleansed them from leprosy (Luke 17: 11 – 19)? No, the Israelites bowed their heads and worshipped the Lord as recorded in Exodus 12:27. Why did they worship the Lord? The Israelites worshipped the Lord because they knew what could wash away their sins and make them whole again. Nothing but the blood of Jesus as cited in 1 John 1: 7. In essence, the Israelites were not concerned about death. They overcame Pharoah by the blood of the lamb and the word of their testimony. They knew there is power in the blood as illustrated in a song by Shirley Caesar.

## Key Point 3:

Thirdly, let's look at the power of the Passover. In one moment, day, or night, the power of the Lord can turn your life around just like he did for the Israelites. This is illustrated in Exodus 12: 29. It reads, "And it came to pass that at midnight the Lord smote all the firstborn in the land of Egypt, from the firstborn of Pharaoh that sat on his throne unto the firstborn of the captive that was in the dungeon; and all the firstborn of cattle."

When the enemy sees that you have victory through the Lord, Satan will get behind thee (Matthew 16: 23). This was the case with Pharoah. After 10 plagues (not 1, not 2, not 3), he finally got the message to let God's people go as recorded in Exodus 12: 30 – 31. It reads "And Pharaoh rose up in the night, he, and all his servants, and all the Egyptians; and there was a great cry in Egypt; for there was not a house where there was not one dead. And he called for Moses and Aaron by night, and said, Rise up, and get you forth from among my people, both ye and the children of Israel; and go serve the Lord, as ye have said." In other words, go quickly or expeditiously Israelites. I finally got the message. I was selfish, stubborn, stupid, asinine, foolish, brainless, mindless, unethical, uncouth, uncivilized, and evil but I finally got the message. I was Johnny comes lately; so go and serve the God of Abraham, Isaiah, and Jacob!

I'm curious, Brother Ronald. What lessons are to be learned from this story about the Israelites? One lesson to be learned is that we don't have to get upset with people who do us wrong. The Lord has a way of turning things around such as making the enemy our footstool (Psalm 110: 1). A second lesson to be learned is that we must always praise the Lord. The bible says, "let everything that has breath praise the Lord" (Psalm 150:6). A third lesson to be learned is that we must serve the Lord who woke us this morning, brought us from a mighty long way, saved our life, healed our bodies, put joy in our heart, and peace in our soul. Another lesson to be learned is that we must serve the Lord who died on the cross for our sins, so we can live again. We must remember to ask the Lord to have mercy on us as we sing "Pass me not, O gentle Savior. Hear my humble cry. While on others thou art calling, do not pass me by." We must remember to thank God for all His blessings. He delivered the Israelites from bondage, and that's The Promise of the Passover.

A final lesson to be learned from this story is that we don't have to worry about the troubles of the world. We take our troubles to the Lord because He is bigger than the universe. He is bigger than the sun and stars. He is bigger than the things that can tear us apart. He is bigger than the earth and death. He is bigger than HIV and financial insecurity. He is bigger than negativity and calamity as illustrated in another song by Jekalyn Carr. Take a listen to the song.

In summary, First Timothy, this lesson focused on the preparation of the Passover, the purpose of the Passover, and the power of the Passover. Jesus can and will take care of us. He is the mighty God because He has all power in His hand. He delivered the Israelites from bondage, and that's The Promise of the Passover. Thus, I leave you with three questions: (1) Do you believe the power of the blood? (2) Do you have a testimony from God? (3) How have you used your testimony from God? Amen.

At this time, let's reflect on some of the daily journal questions on the "Passover" from the book, "Beyond the Sunday Sermon." Constance Holmes will lead the discussion.

We are now at the end of bible study. We certainly hope you have gained something from this bible study. We look forward to your participation in next Wednesday's lesson titled The Power of Living on "Yet" (Pages 255 – 260) from the book *"Beyond the Sunday Sermon."* The scriptures are: Job 13: 15; Habakkuk 2:2-3; Zechariah 8:20,23; and Romans 8:25. If you would like to read some news articles about the bible study at First Timothy, go to the website of The Holmes Education Post.

Finally, we encourage you to invite a guest to our bible study in church or online. If we have any visitors in church tonight, please raise your hand so we can acknowledge your presence. We thank you for attending bible study with us. We encourage you to come again.

Now, we will have closing remarks from Reverend Newbill.

*A 12 Week Bible Study from the Devotional Book "Beyond the Sunday Sermon"*

# WEEK 9: Outline of Service

Outline of Service
First Timothy Wednesday Night Bible Study
November 1, 2023
7:00PM – 8:00PM

Message: The Promise of the Passover
from the book *"Beyond the Sunday Sermon"* (Pages 249 - 254)
Scripture: Exodus 12:13, 21 - 31 KJV

| Time | What | By Whom | Music to play or Visual to Display |
|---|---|---|---|
| 6:53PM – 7:00PM | Song/video: I'll Just Say Yes by Brian Courtney Wilson (7:01) | Media Ministry to play song/video | • Play song/music – I'll Just Say Yes |
| 7:00PM -7:02PM | Prayer and Intro of Wednesday Night Bible Study | Rev. Newbill or Minister Milton | • Show Slide 1 – Wednesday Night Bible Study |
| 7:02PM – 7:05PM | Intro & Teaching Method | Dr. Ronald Holmes | • Show Slide 2 – God's Promises |
| 7:05PM – 7:10PM | Reading the Excerpt of Sunday Sermon & Scripture | Constance Holmes | • Slide 3 – The Promise of Passover |
| 7:10PM – 7:15PM | • Three Key Points from the Message<br>• Constance's Travel<br>• Point #1 – The Preparation | Dr. Ronald Holmes | • Slide 4/5/6 (Key Points, Constance Travel, Point #1-The Preparation |
| 7:15PM –7:20PM | Song/Video:<br>• I Believe God – Jekalyn Carr (4:57) | Media Ministry to play music video | • Slide 7 to show until music video starts playing<br>• Play music video/ song –I Believe God |
| 7:20PM –7:23PM | • Point #2 – Purpose of the Passover | Dr. Ronald Holmes | • Slide 8 – Point# 2-Purpose of the Passover |

| 7:23PM – 7:26PM | Song/Video:<br>• There is Power in the Blood – Shirley Caesar (2:50) | Media Ministry to play music video | • Play Slide 9 until music video starts<br>• Play music/video – There is Power in the Blood |
|---|---|---|---|
| 7:26PM – 7:28 | • Point #3 -The Power of Passover | Dr. Ronald Holmes | • Slide 10 – Point #3 The Power of Passover |
| 7:28PM –7:36PM | • Song/Video: You're Bigger – Jekalyn Carr (7:38) | Media Ministry to play music video | • Slide 11 to show until music video starts<br>• Play music video/song – You're Bigger |
| 7:36PM – 7:38PM | • Summarize Three Key Points | Dr. Ronald Holmes | • Slide 12 – Summary of Key Points |
| 7:38PM – 7:53PM | Facilitated discussion of Daily Journal from the Book-Pages 252 - 254 | Constance Holmes | • Slides 13 - 16 - as each question is being discussed |
| 7:53PM – 7:56PM | Summary of Bible Study | Dr. Ronald Holmes | • Slide 17 & 18 |
| 7:56PM – 8:00PM | Closing Comments & Prayer | Reverend Newbill or Minister Milton | • Continue with Slide 19 |

- I'll Just Say Yes- https://www.youtube.com/watch?v=mZ_sMqDYWj8
- I Believe God – https://youtu.be/1ZxoEC4H4Rw?si=GB7kFM3e215Kx37r
- There is Power in the Blood - https://youtu.be/hSLN6WZc344?si=SumfryzEj655Rwj
- You're Bigger - https://youtu.be/Z_ZV61eDLXI?si=jawBJGjtfRSa_WSW

*A 12 Week Bible Study from the Devotional Book "Beyond the Sunday Sermon"*

# WEEK 9: Visual Slides

Key Messages about the Promise of the Passover

The Preparation   The Purpose   The Power

Ronald W. Holmes, Ph.D.

1. Preparation of the Passover

Constance's Travel Route

2. The Purpose of the Passover

110

*A 12 Week Bible Study from the Devotional Book "Beyond the Sunday Sermon"*

Shirley Caesar

There is Power in the Blood

Jekalyn Carr

You're Bigger

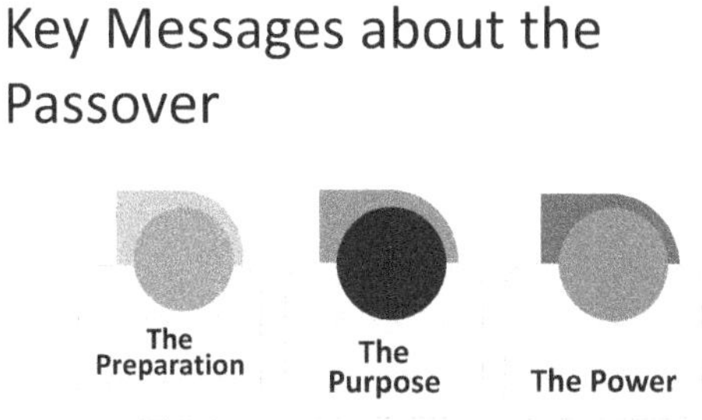

## Key Messages about the Passover

The Preparation

The Purpose

The Power

JOURNAL DISCUSSION:

THE PROMISE OF THE PASSOVER

111

Ronald W. Holmes, Ph.D.

**Question #1**

What is the meaning of "leavened bread" which was not to be eaten by the Israelites?

**Question #2**

Discuss how we can be cleansed from our sins.

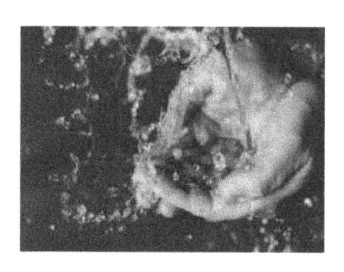

**Question #3**

What messages of promise do you take from this Passover story?

Next Wednesday's Bible Study

The Power of Living on "Yet"
Pages 255 - 260

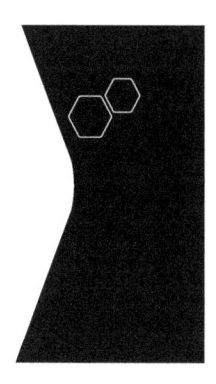

*A 12 Week Bible Study from the Devotional Book "Beyond the Sunday Sermon"*

## Closing REMARKS

## WEEK 10

# The Power of Living on "Yet"

I hope you are hungry – This is how the waitresses would greet customers at my favorite Atlanta restaurant, Okay Café, before ordering their food. In the same vein, I hope you are hungry before I give the lesson on The Power of Living on "Yet." Good evening, Reverend Frederick Newbill, members, friends, and guest of First Timothy Baptist Church. Thank you for joining us today for Wednesday Night Bible Study.

The word "Yet" refers to something that will or may happen in the foreseeable future. Let me provide a few examples of "Yet." I haven't told anybody else yet. Please don't go yet. Aren't you ready to jog yet? This class was the best yet. I haven't joined the church yet. I didn't get a raise yet. I'm not married yet. I'm not on Facebook yet. I'm not healed yet. I'm not tired yet. I have a "yet" faith. What is a "yet" faith? Thanks for asking.

"Yet" faith is when we go through tribulations such as a death, sickness, crisis, hardship, unemployment, torment, epidemic, or pandemic; but we still trust God. "Yet" faith is a declaration that we ride or die with God. "Yet" faith means that no matter what people think, do, or say, we still trust God. "Yet" faith means we may never be able to explain, how a black cow eats green grass and produces white milk; we just believe that God is able.

Can you give two examples of "yet" faith? Yes, when Shadrack, Meshach, and Abednego refused to bow down to King Nebuchadnezzar and determined to die for their faith, that was a "yet" faith experience as recorded in Daniel 3: 16 – 18.

When "Jesus cried out with a loud voice, My God, My God – why hast thou forsaken me?" (Matthew 27:46) and then said, "Father into your hands, I commend my spirit" (Luke 23: 46) – that was a "yet" faith experience.

With that said, this lesson will highlight The Power of Living on "Yet" or "Yet" faith rather than the power of living on positions, prestige, money, and wealth.

Using our teaching style for this bible study, we are going to (1) read an excerpt of the Sunday Sermon and Scripture from the book titled *"Beyond the Sunday Sermon;"* (2) discuss the three key points from the Sunday Sermon lesson; (3) provide concrete details to support the key points; and (4) summarize the lesson with scriptures and questions from the daily journal. Constance Holmes will come and read the excerpt of the lesson and scripture.

Thank you, Constance. Now, let's look closely at the three key points for today's lesson. The lesson highlights The Power of Living on "yet" or "yet" faith by encouraging people to (1) trust God's power, (2) trust God's presence, and (3) trust God promises.

Ronald W. Holmes, Ph.D.

## Key Point 1:

We must exercise our "yet" faith, follow God, and trust the power of him just as God has done for the saints in the past. In Zechariah 8:20 – 23, for example, people from different cities, countries, and powerful nations came to Jerusalem to worship the mighty God and seek his help. Ten men from all languages and nations took hold of one Jew by the hem of His robe and said, let us go with you because "we heard that God is with you."

If we turn to God and trust his power, he can turn bad situations into good situations. He can do things that no man can do. He can do things we can't see today, yet if we trust the power of the mighty God, he can still do the impossible. With him, "all things are possible" (Matthew 19: 26). Remember, He fed 5,000 with two fish and five loaves of bread (Matthew 14: 17 – 21). If we trust the power of God, He can feed us when our body is hungry or thirsty for the living word of God. If we trust the power of God with a "yet faith," he can turn our darkness into light. He can turn our sadness into gladness.

Remember, He healed the woman who bled for 12 years. She had a "yet' faith mentality. The woman said, "If I may but touch his garment, I shall be whole" (Matthew 9:20 – 22). Remember, he abled blind Bartimaeus to see. Bartimaeus refused to be persuaded by the people in Jericho and adamantly asked Jesus to have mercy on him (Mark 10: 48). Jesus, the mighty God, said in Matthew 28: 18, "All power is given unto me in heaven and earth."

Thus, we must know that we are living because of the power of God. God's power is with us, in us, and through us. We must know that "greater is he that is in us than he that is in the world" (1 John 4: 4). We must know that we are God's children; and we will become like him when he returns to the world (1 John 3: 2). We must know that we are here on earth not by our might but by the spirit and power of the Lord (Zechariah 4: 6). God can enable us to overcome any hardship in life. The "yet" faith mentality means no matter what people do to us, we never quit, we never say die, and we never throw in the towel, so to speak. As an example, take a listen to a scene from the movie Men of Honor, "Don't let him up until he stops moving."

This was a true story of Carl Brashear, played by Cuba Gooding Jr., who exemplified the "yet" faith mentality to become a Navy Diver under difficult circumstances. To become a Navy diver, they had to assemble a flange underwater using a bag of tools. It took one man 1:37; a second man 2:19; and a third man 4:09 to complete the task. It took Carl 9:31 to complete the task because the chief punched a hole in his tool bag before sending it to him. To be successful, Carl had to collect the pieces that were scattered from the tool bag on the river bottom before he could assemble the flange.

## Key Point 2:

Secondly, we must trust God's presence 365 days a year and know that he lives in us, and "we dwell in him" (1 John 4: 13). It is a known fact that in this world we are going to have trials and tribulations; but we must be of good cheer because the Lord "has overcome the world" (John 16:33). We must live our life, maintain our praise, and worship the presence of the Lord with a "yet" faith mentality. Job provides another example of a "yet" faith experience. As recorded in Job 1: 13 – 19, he lost his children, animals, and property. Job said, "Though he slay me, yet will I trust in him, but I will maintain mine own ways before him" (Job 13:15).

As horrible as Job's situation was, this was a testament that the Lord "will never leave us nor forsake us" (Hebrews 13:5). This was a testament that the Lord will never put no more on us than we can handle (1 Corinthians 10: 13). Job wholeheartedly trusted the presence of the Lord. When things appeared overwhelming, Job's wife told him to curse God and die. Job responded to his wife; you talk like a foolish woman (Job 2: 9-10). Job clearly had a "yet" faith mentality. He said in Job 19: 25 – 26, (verse 25) "For I know my Redeemer liveth; and he shall stand at the latter day upon the earth; (verse 26) and though after my skin worms destroy my body; yet in my flesh shall I see God."

I can hear Job saying, because he lives, I can face tomorrow; all my fear is gone, and life is worth the living just because he lives. I know he is going to come through for me in my darkness hour. I know he will carry me through as I just trust in his word. While using some words from the song (My God is Real), I can hear Job saying, God is real in my soul; but there are some things I may not know. There are some places Oh Lord, I cannot go. But I am sure of this one thing, you are real. For I can feel you in my soul. Yes, God you are real. For you have washed and made me whole. Ooh, your love for me is just like pure gold. I can feel you in my soul while living on the "yet" faith mentality. God says to Job and all of us "lo I be with you always until the end of the world" if you obey my commandments (Matthew 28: 20).

While using words from another song (The Presence of the Lord is Here), I can hear Job saying the presence, spirit, power, and blessing of the Lord is here, I can feel it in the atmosphere. Everybody blows the trumpets and sound the alarm. Because the Lord is in the Temple, let everybody bow. Let all the people praise him now! Take a Listen to this song by Byron Cage.

## Key Point 3:

Thirdly, we must learn how to trust God's promises for ourselves. If family members, church members, and friends don't pray or trust God, we must continue to trust him for ourselves. We must get our own spiritual high and not depend on somebody else to grow spiritually with the Lord for us as well as have a relationship with the Lord for us. We must individually have a relationship with God and trust his promises. For all of God's promises are "yes" and "amen" to the glory of him as recorded in 2 Corinthians 1:20. As a new year resolution (it's getting close to that time), we might decide to stand or continue to stand on the "yet" faith of God's promises. We might also decide to write our goals to develop a book or start a business. In fact, Sister Osborne is coordinating a workshop for writing a book at First Timothy on November 16 at 6:00p.m. In planning, we must write our vision, make it plain, and wait for it to materialize as recorded in Habakkuk 2:2-3. "For we are saved by hope" through Jesus Christ our Lord and Savior as recorded in Romans 8:24. For instance, we did not see July 2023, until it came. We were hoping that we would be here when it came; but we could not rush God to bring July in January. God causes us to wait patiently for what we don't presently see or have. Some of us had to wait patiently for the things that mean the most to us such as a friend, wife, husband, son, daughter, pet, job, paycheck, credit card, cell phone, vehicle, vacation, apartment, house, and insurance. As we wait for something, we are mindful of the word "yet" and its uses such as: I have not connected with the friend yet. I'm not married yet. I have not bought a pet yet. I have not found a job yet.

As mentioned earlier, "Yet" is a powerful word that refers to something that will or may happen in the foreseeable future. God is not finished with me yet. Through our "yet" faith mentality, God will bring our vision to fruition if we trust his promises and have patience in him. God works in mysterious ways. His wonders to perform. We know that at midnight God does some of his best work as noted in the story of the Israelites. Remember, at midnight, "God struck down all the firstborn in the land of Egypt from the oldest child of Pharoah sitting on his throne to the oldest child of the prisoner in jail; and the firstborn of the animals" (Exodus 12: 29). God does some of his best work at night. That's the reason we can sing, "Weeping may endure for a night, but joy cometh in the morning" (Psalm 30: 5).

I Love You, Lord. In the darkest night you are close like no other. Your mercy never fails me. From the moment that I wake, until I lay my head to sleep. All my life (Lord) you have been so good to me as a father and friend. All my life (Lord) you have been faithful; so with every breath that I am able, I will sing of the goodness of God by Cece Winans. Take a Listen to the song.

In summary, First Timothy, this lesson highlighted The Power of Living on "Yet" or "Yet" faith by encouraging people to (1) trust God's power; (2) trust God's presence; and (3) trust God's promises. As we practice and maintain a "yet faith" mentality like the woman with the issue of blood, Job, and Bartimaeus, we "can do all things through Christ which strengtheneths us" (Philippians 4: 13). Thus, I leave with you three questions: (1) What has been your "yet" faith experience? (2) Have you shared your "yet" faith experience with someone? (3) How did you feel after sharing your "yet" faith experience? Amen.

At this time, let's reflect on some of the daily journal questions on Faith" from the book, *"Beyond the Sunday Sermon."* Constance Holmes will lead the discussion.

We are now at the end of our 10th bible study. We certainly hope you have gained something from this bible study. We look forward to your participation in next Wednesday's lesson titled, Trust in God (Pages 261 - 266) from the book *"Beyond the Sunday Sermon."* The scripture is Psalms 118: 1-9. This will be the last bible study in November before the Thanksgiving Holiday.

On Wednesday, December 6, the lesson is titled Remember, Repent, Return, and Respect (Pages 180 – 184). The scripture is Revelation 2: 1-7. This will be the last bible study in December before the Christmas Holiday.

We encourage you to invite a guest to our bible study in church or online. If we have any visitors in church tonight, please raise your hand so we can acknowledge your presence. We thank you for your attendance. We encourage you to come again.

Now, we will have closing remarks from Reverend Newbill.

*Ronald W. Holmes, Ph.D.*

# WEEK 10: Outline of Service

Outline of Service
First Timothy Wednesday Night Bible Study
November 8, 2023
7:00PM – 8:00PM

Message: The Power of Living on Yet
from the book *"Beyond the Sunday Sermon"* (Pages 255 - 260)
Scripture: Job 13:15; Habakkuk 2:2-3: Zechariah 8:20, 23; Roman 8:25 KJV

| Time | What | By Whom | Music to play or Visual to Display |
|---|---|---|---|
| 6:53PM – 7:00PM | Song/video: I'll Just Say Yes by Brian Courtney Wilson (7:01) | Media Ministry to play song/ video | • Play song/music – I'll Just Say Yes |
| 7:00PM -7:02PM | Prayer and Intro of Wednesday Night Bible Study | Rev. Newbill or Minister Milton | • Show Slide 1 – Wednesday Night Bible Study |
| 7:02PM – 7:05PM | Intro & Teaching Method | Dr. Ronald Holmes | • Show Slide 2– The Power of Living on Yet |
| 7:05PM – 7:10PM | Reading the Excerpt – The Power of Living on Yet | Constance Holmes | • Slide 3 – Believe in the Power of Yet |
| 7:10PM – 7:15PM | • Three Key Points from the Message<br>• Point #1 Exercise Our Yet Faith | Dr. Ronald Holmes | • Slide 4 -Key Messages<br>• Slide 5 – Point #1 – Exercise our Yet Faith |
| 7:15PM –7:18PM | Video:<br>• Men of Honor Video Clip - Til He Stops Moving (2:42) | Media Ministry to play music video | • Slide 6 - to show slide until video starts playing<br>• Play Video – Men of Honor – Til He Stops Moving |
| 7:18PM –7:21PM | • Point #2 – Trust God's Presence | Dr. Ronald Holmes | • Slide 7 – Point# 2-Trust God's Presence |

*A 12 Week Bible Study from the Devotional Book "Beyond the Sunday Sermon"*

| 7:21PM – 7:28PM | Song/Video:<br>• The Presence of the Lord – Byron Cage (13:38 -**STOP at 7:21**) | Media Ministry to play music video | • Play Slide 8 until music video starts<br>• Play music/video – The Presence of the Lord – **Stop at 7:21** |
|---|---|---|---|
| 7:28PM – 7:32 | • Point #3 -Trust God's Promises | Dr. Ronald Holmes | • Slide 9 – Point #3 Trust God's Promises |
| 7:32PM –7:37PM | • Song/Video: Goodness of God – CeCe Winans (4:55) | Media Ministry to play music video | • Slide 10 to show until music video starts<br>• Play music video/song – Goodness of God |
| 7:37PM – 7:38PM | • Summarize Three Key Points | Dr. Ronald Holmes | • Slide 11– Summary of Key Points |
| 7:38PM – 7:53PM | Facilitated discussion of Daily Journal from the Book-Pages 258- 260 | Constance Holmes | • Slides 12 - 15 - as each question is being discussed |
| 7:53PM – 7:56PM | Next Week's Bible Study | Dr. Ronald Holmes | • Slide 16/17 |
| 7:56PM – 8:00PM | Closing Comments & Prayer | Reverend Newbill or Minister Milton | • Continue with Slide 18 |

- I'll Just Say Yes- https://www.youtube.com/watch?v=mZ_sMqDYWj8
- Men of Honor Video - https://youtu.be/FixQE61iSDg?si=_xmGYUNgaHYj7-3P
- The Presence of the Lord - https://youtu.be/2OpO6EL2kbM?si=yjtD5d8co7Jx8nMA
- Goodness of God - https://youtu.be/9sE5kEnitqE?si=Ayp1-HXSmWx6xVxr

# WEEK 10: Visual Slides

**The Power of Living on "YET"**

Key Messages:
Living on "Yet" Faith, Trust God's

Power   Presence   Promises

*A 12 Week Bible Study from the Devotional Book "Beyond the Sunday Sermon"*

1. Exercise Our "YET" Faith

2. Trust God's Presence

Byron Cage
The Presence of
the Lord is Here

3. Trust God's Promises

CeCe Winans
Goodness of God

Key Messages:
Living on "Yet" Faith, Trust God's

Power   Presence   Promises

JOURNAL DISCUSSION:

THE POWER OF LIVING ON "YET"

*A 12 Week Bible Study from the Devotional Book "Beyond the Sunday Sermon"*

**Question #1**

Discuss your experience when you "walked by faith, not by sight."

**Question #2**

Discuss your understanding of how all things are possible through God.

**Question #3**

Why is charity the greatest among the three (faith, hope, charity)?

# Next Wednesday's Bible Study

Trust in God
Pages 261 - 266

127

*Ronald W. Holmes, Ph.D.*

Bible Study Calendar for Rest of Year

- November 15
- December 6
- December 13

**NOVEMBER 2023**

**DECEMBER 2023**

# Closing REMARKS

## WEEK 11

# Trust in God

We've come this far by faith. Leaning on the Lord. Trusting in His holy word. He has never failed me yet. Good evening, Reverend Frederick Newbill, members, friends, and guest of First Timothy Baptist Church. We welcome you to Wednesday Night Bible Study for the lesson on "Trust in God."

Who are you going to call when you are faced with tribulations? Is it Ghostbuster, Superman, Spiderman, Mosquito Man, Catwoman, or Superwoman? Who are you going to call when you are faced with distress, duress, and unrest? Who are you going to trust when you have had enough of the troubles in the world? Considering the times that we are living, this lesson will focus on why we must Trust in God.

Using our teaching style for this bible study, we are going to (1) read an excerpt of the Sunday Sermon and Scripture from the book titled *"Beyond the Sunday Sermon;"* (2) discuss the three key points from the Sunday Sermon lesson; (3) provide concrete details to support the key points; and (4) summarize the lesson with scriptures and questions from the daily journal. Constance Holmes will come and read the excerpt of the lesson and scripture.

Thank you, Constance. Now, let's look closely at the three key points for today's lesson on why we must "Trust in God." They include (1) magnifying the mercy of God, (2) a testimony over triumph in troubles, and (3) confessing confidence in the Lord.

## Key Point 1:

We must trust God because of his amazing grace, favor, and tender mercy for trouble will come and go in our life. There is no age requirement for trouble. There is no course you can take to outrun or escape trouble. Things will fail us in life such as appliances, automobiles, cellular phones, computers, airplanes, and trains. Our bodies will fail us. People will fail us too.

The bible says in Psalm 118:8, "It is better to trust in the Lord than to put confidence in man." If we want to find peace in troubling times, we must learn how to trust and obey the Lord. A songwriter Barry Collecutt says, "When we walk with the Lord, in the light of his word, what a glory he sheds on our way. While we do his good will, he abides with us still; and with all who will trust and obey. Trust and obey for there's no other way to be happy in Jesus; but to trust and obey; Not a shadow can rise, not a cloud in the skies; but his smile quickly drives it away. Not a doubt or a fear, not a sigh or a tear, can abide while we trust and obey."

Another songwriter Luther Barnes says, "Trouble in my way. I got to cry sometimes. I lay awake at night but that's alright. Jesus will fix it after while."

The bible says, "O give thanks unto the Lord; for he is good: for his mercy endureth forever" (Psalm 136: 1). The bible also says let Israel; the house of Aaron; and those who fear the Lord say his mercy endureth forever (Psalm 118: 1-4).

How many of you have experienced trouble in your life? How many of you fear God and can give thanks to God for he is good and his mercy endureth forever? God is the only one we can trust in our life because he is "Alpha and Omega, the beginning and ending, and the Almighty" (Revelation 1:8). His mercy endureth forever. Honey drippers will not endure forever. Ice cream cones will not endure forever. Popsicles will not endure forever. Popcorn will not endure forever. Your beautiful smile will not endure forever. Your 401K will not endure forever; but God's mercy will endure forever.

Thus, we must magnify, appreciate, and confirm the living truth that if it had not been for the mercy of God, where would we be. We must thank God for his mercies. "It is of the Lord's mercies that we are not consumed because his compassions fail not. They are new every morning: great is thy faithfulness" (Lamentations 3: 22-23). Because of God's love, kindness, grace, and tender mercy, I can see day after day. Take a listen to "Great is Your Mercy" by Donnie McClurkin!

## Key Point 2:

Secondly, I heard a songwriter sing, "As I look back over my life and think things over, I can truly say I have been blessed; I have a testimony." However, we can't have a testimony without a test. We can't have victory unless we have been a victim. For example, David was faced with a troubling situation of fighting Goliath, a much stronger and bigger man. David was able to defeat Goliath because of his faith and trust in God.

Do you have faith and trust in God? Do you have a testimony? God will allow some test in our life to be a testimony for someone else. I'm reminded of story about three little boys. Can I tell you the story? Okay. These boys went to a grocery store and applied for a job. The manager asked the first boy, why do you want the job? The first boy said, "I want the job so I can buy me a bicycle." The manager asked the second boy, why do you want the job? The second boy said, "I want the job so I can buy me a BB gun." The manager asked the third boy, why do you want the job? But before the boy could respond to the question, tears started pouring down his face; so the manager asked the boy, why are you crying son? The boy said, "My mama and daddy got killed in an accident when I was a little baby boy; and nobody raised me but Grandma." Now, my Grandma has gotten old. She gets sick sometimes. Sometimes, she can't get out of the bed. Sometimes she can't cook anything. Sometimes, I have to help Grandma walk. Sometimes, I have to help Grandma take her medicine; so I want the job to help Grandma pay our bills. Grandma has been so good to me. She has been a mother to me. She has been a father to me. She has given me everything I asked for over the years. She has always prayed for me; so I want the job to help my Grandma. What a testimony. That boy got the job and helped his Grandma.

Do you have a testimony? Have you helped somebody? As we experience triumph over our trials and tribulations, we will have a testimony to inspire others to trust in God. What God did for one person, he can do the same for another person. When we go through some test in life, we will be able to tell people about how we were able to overcome the test. We can't tell people about mental health such as bipolar disorder if we have not experienced it; so when we are faced with a test such as distress, duress, and unrest, who are we going to call?

David said, "I called upon the Lord in distress," he answered me, and set me free as recorded in Psalm 118:5. With today's technology, First Timothy, people can disappoint you when you call upon them. When they see that you are trying to call them, they can ignore the call and text; but we must remember to call upon the Lord in distress. In fact, Jeremiah 33: 3 says call upon the Lord and he will answer you and show you greater and mighty things that you have never seen before. In fact, Psalm 118:6 says, when "the Lord is on my side; I will not fear: What can man do unto me?" As believers, we say, absolutely nothing! Because the Lord is a very present help in the time of trouble. He will enable us to be victorious over those who hate us as recorded in Psalm 118:7. Has anybody experienced some hate? Has anybody been misunderstood? Has anybody been falsely criticized? Has anybody faced some trouble?

If yes, we must remember to "trust the Lord than to put confidence in man" (Psalm 118: 8). We must remember that "no weapon formed against thee shall prosper" (Isaiah 54:17). We must remember that the God we serve will prepare a table in the midst of our enemies (Psalm 23:5). We must remember that the Lord will make our enemies our footstool (Psalm 110:1). Do I have a witness?

As I said earlier, we can't have a testimony without a test. We can't have victory unless we have been a victim. As an example, take a listen to a Diner scene from the movie Glory Road.

As you heard, the men had to retrain themselves so they could have a testimony for someone else. This movie was based on true events leading to the 1966 NCAA Men's Division I Basketball Tournament where Texas Western College defeated Kentucky for the National Championship by starting all Black players. This was the first time ever done in history and symbolized solidarity and hope after a season facing discrimination. This was a Goliath type situation that threatened the humanity, dignity, and safety of the Black players; but they held steadfast during distress, duress, and unrest and accomplished the impossible.

## Key Point 3:

Thirdly, we must confess, trust, and "place our confidence in the Lord" rather than man (Psalm 118: 8-9). With man, salvation is impossible; "but with God all things are possible" (Matthew 19: 26). David defeated Goliath which appeared to be impossible. He knew the battle was the Lord's and not his own (1 Samuel 17: 45-47). David knew he "can do all things through Christ which strengtheneth" him (Philippians 4:13). He knew that "greater is he that is in me than he that is in the world" (1 John 4: 4).

As a blessing, all we need in this world is the Lord. All power is given unto to him "in heaven and earth" (Matthew 28:18). "His name shall be called Wonderful, Counsellor, the Mighty God, the Everlasting Father, and the Prince of Peace" (Isaiah 9: 6). He is Wonderful in his power to allow us to attend bible study tonight. He is a Counselor because he has all the answers to our questions. He is the Mighty God because He is "the way, truth, and the life" (John 14: 6).

He the Everlasting Father because we have someone that death could not kill. Jesus is the Prince of Peace because he was anointed by God to save us from our sins and offer us eternal life. As a blessing, all we need in this world is "to trust the Lord with all our heart" and don't depend on our own understanding. In all our ways, acknowledge him, and he shall direct our paths. (Proverbs 3: 5-6). As a blessing, all we need to know is that God is Good as sang by Jonathan McReynolds. Take a listen to the song.

In summary, this lesson focused on three key points on why we must "Trust in God." They include (1) magnifying the mercy of God, (2) a testimony over triumph in troubles, and (3) confessing confidence in the Lord. God is the answer to everything we need in this world. We must seek, trust, and follow his commandments. Amen.

At this time, let's reflect on some of the daily journal questions on Endureth" from the book, *"Beyond the Sunday Sermon."* Constance Holmes will lead the discussion.

We are now at the end of the bible study. We certainly hope you have gained something from this bible study. We look forward to your participation in our last bible study for 2023 on Wednesday, December 6. The lesson is titled, Remember, Repent, Return, and Respect (Pages 180 – 184). The scripture is Revelation 2: 1-7.

We encourage you to invite a guest to our bible study in church or online. If we have any visitors in church tonight, please raise your hand so we can acknowledge your presence. We thank you for your attendance. We encourage you to come again. Enjoy your Thanksgiving Holiday.

Now, we will have closing remarks from Minister Milton.

*Ronald W. Holmes, Ph.D.*

# WEEK 11: Outline of Service

Outline of Service
First Timothy Wednesday Night Bible Study
November 15, 2023
7:00PM – 8:00PM

Message: Trust in God
from the book *"Beyond the Sunday Sermon"* (Pages 261 - 266)
Scripture: Psalms 118:1-9 KJV

| Time | What | By Whom | Music to play or Visual to Display |
|---|---|---|---|
| 6:53PM – 7:00PM | Song/video: I'll Just Say Yes by Brian Courtney Wilson (7:01) | Media Ministry to play song/video | • Play song/music – I'll Just Say Yes |
| 7:00PM -7:02PM | Prayer and Intro of Wednesday Night Bible Study | Rev. Newbill or Minister Milton | • Show Slide 1 – Wednesday Night Bible Study |
| 7:02PM – 7:05PM | Intro & Teaching Method | Dr. Ronald Holmes | • Show Slide 2– Trust in God |
| 7:05PM – 7:10PM | Reading the Excerpt – Trust in God | Constance Holmes | • Slide 2 – Trust in God |
| 7:10PM – 7:15PM | • Three Key Points from the Message<br>• Point #1 – Magnifying the Mercy of God | Dr. Ronald Holmes | • Slide 3 -Key Messages<br>• Slide 4 – Magnifying the Mercy of God |
| 7:15PM –7:21PM | Song/Video:<br>• Great is Your Mercy – Donnie McClurkin (6:00) | Media Ministry to play music video | • Slide 5 - to show slide until video starts playing<br>• Play Music Video – Great is Your Mercy |
| 7:21PM –7:25PM | • Point #2 – A Testimony Over Triumph in Troubles | Dr. Ronald Holmes | • Slide 6 – Point# 2-Testimony over Triumph in Troubles |
| 7:25PM – 7:28PM | Video:<br>• Glory Road – 2:50 | Media Ministry to play music video | • Play Slide 7 until music video starts<br>• Play Video – Glory Road |

*A 12 Week Bible Study from the Devotional Book "Beyond the Sunday Sermon"*

| | | | |
|---|---|---|---|
| 7:28PM – 7:30 | • Point #3 -Confessing Confidence in the Lord | Dr. Ronald Holmes | • Slide 8 – Point #3 Confessing Confidence in the Lord |
| 7:30PM –7:33PM | • Song/Video: God is Good – Jonathan McReynolds (3:21) | Media Ministry to play music video | • Slide 9 to show until music video starts<br>• Play music video/song – God is Good |
| 7:33PM – 7:34PM | • Summarize Three Key Points | Dr. Ronald Holmes | • Slide 10– Summary of Key Points |
| 7:34PM – 7:53PM | Facilitated discussion of Daily Journal from the Book-Pages 264- 266 | Constance Holmes | • Slides 11 - 14 - as each question is being discussed |
| 7:53PM – 7:56PM | Next Week's Bible Study | Dr. Ronald Holmes | • Slide 15/16 |
| 7:56PM – 8:00PM | Closing Comments & Prayer | Reverend Newbill or Minister Milton | • Continue with Slide 17 |

- I'll Just Say Yes- https://www.youtube.com/watch?v=mZ_sMqDYWj8
- Great is Your Mercy - https://youtu.be/A-cAfUPMHxk?si=7Jv_ffYD_tA3UyiJ
- Glory Road - https://youtu.be/W2ewRXN8aeM
- God is Good- https://youtu.be/-f9uGdJYPeA?si=7x7zh7pPsjA1XvT2

Ronald W. Holmes, Ph.D.

# WEEK 11: Visual Slides

**WELCOME TO FIRST TIMOTHY**
Wednesday Night Bible Study

**Trust in God**

### Key Points
- Magnifying the mercy of God
- A testimony over triumph in troubles
- Confessing confidence in the Lord

**1. Magnifying the Mercy of God**

138

*A 12 Week Bible Study from the Devotional Book "Beyond the Sunday Sermon"*

Donnie McClurkin

Great is Your Mercy

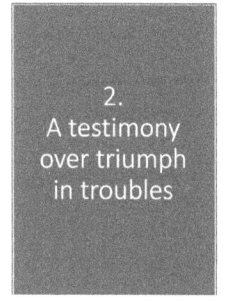

2. A testimony over triumph in troubles

GLORY ROAD

3. Confessing confidence in the Lord

*Ronald W. Holmes, Ph.D.*

## Jonathan McReynolds

## God is Good

### Key Points

**Trust in God**

- Magnifying the mercy of God
- A testimony over triumph in troubles
- Confessing confidence in the Lord

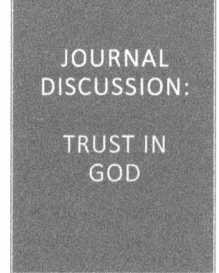

### JOURNAL DISCUSSION: TRUST IN GOD

**Question #1**

Discuss how the Lord has blessed your family from generation to generation.

*A 12 Week Bible Study from the Devotional Book "Beyond the Sunday Sermon"*

### Question #2

What are some reasons you give thanks to the Lord for his mercy?

### Question #3

Discuss how you maintained your faith in the Lord during the evils of humankind.

## Next Wednesday's Bible Study

Remember, Repent, Return and Respect
Pages 180 - 184

Last Bible Study of 2023

December 6

## Closing REMARKS

## WEEK 12

# Remember, Repent, Return & Respect

"He that hath an ear, let him hear what the spirit saith" (Revelation 2:7). Good evening, members, friends, and guest of First Timothy Baptist Church. On behalf of our pastor Reverend Frederick Douglas Newbill, Sr., we welcome you to Wednesday Night Bible Study for the lesson on "Remember, Repent, Return, & Respect." We would like to dedicate this bible study to Reverend Newbill for his unconventional, untiring, and unwavering service of 36 years at First Timothy; and we know behind every great man there is a great woman such as First Lady, Pamela Newbill. Let's give a sounding ovation with love and appreciation for Reverend & Mrs. Newbill.

In this world, we must respect everybody. In 1972, the Staple Singers made it very clear that, "If you disrespect anybody that you run into, how in the world do you think anybody's supposed to respect you. If you don't give a heck about the man with the bible in his hand, y'all just get out the way, and let the gentleman do his thing." In fact, "he that hath an ear, let him hear what the spirit saith." (Revelation 2:7). Respect Yourself; and do what the pastor tells you!

Using our teaching style for this bible study, we are going to (1) read an excerpt of the Sunday Sermon and Scripture from the book titled *"Beyond the Sunday Sermon;"* (2) discuss the three key points from the Sunday Sermon lesson; (3) provide concrete details to support the key points; and (4) summarize the lesson with scriptures and questions from the daily journal. Constance Holmes will come and read the excerpt of the lesson and scripture.

Thank you, Constance. Now, let's look closely at the three key points for today's lesson on Remember, Repent, Return, and Respect. With an emphasis on the church of Ephesus, this lesson focuses on (1) the words of commendation, (2) the words of condemnation, and (3) the words of correction.

## Key Point 1:

Jesus is known to speak to individuals and groups during different seasons, times, and places. For this text, Jesus is speaking to the seven churches in Asia as recorded in Revelation 1:11. One major point the letters from Jesus to the seven churches have in common is each one concluded with a promise from him to the overcomers of these churches as recorded in Revelation 2:7 through 3:22. These are the words of Jesus "who holdeth the seven stars in his right hand, who walketh in the midst of the seven golden candlesticks" (Revelation 2:1). Aren't you glad that Jesus holds us and walks with us? Jesus explains the mystery of the seven stars and seven lampstands. He says, "The seven stars are the angels of the seven churches and the seven candlesticks are the seven churches" (Revelation 1:20).

In Revelation 2:7, Jesus says to the seven churches, as well as the churches of today, "He that hath an ear, let him hear what the spirit saith unto the churches. To him that overcometh will I give to eat of the tree of life, which is in the midst of the paradise of God."

The risen Christ is among us at First Timothy which recently celebrated 63 years of existence. First Timothy is still standing strong under its current pastor Reverend Newbill because the Lord is walking with us. There was an old spiritual song titled *"Walk with me Lord."* Do you want Jesus to walk with you? The song said, Walk with me Lord! Walk with me! While I'm on this tedious journey, I need you, Jesus, to walk with me."

As you know, many veterans at First Timothy, including our pastor, have served in the military to fight for our country. I'm sure they can testify how the Lord has walked with them on the battlefield and brought them back home to celebrate with their families. Sometimes the Lord will walk with you through the kindness of a stranger when you are on the battlefield like the 7th grader who constantly wrote the African American solider Captain Ned Felder during the Vietnam War and recently met him 56 years later as aired on ABC news. Captain Felder said, the first letter he received from the 7th grader was through divine guidance; and "it made him feel good to be able to keep in touch with someone" while in the army. Is there anybody here who wants Jesus to walk with you? Is there anybody here who loves Jesus? Is there is anybody here who loves the church?

As recorded in Revelation 2:2-3, the Lord commended the church of Ephesus for its good works, labour, patience, tolerance, and endurance just as he commends First Timothy under the leadership of Reverend Newbill for its good works, labour, patience, tolerance, endurance, and participation in ministries to support the needs of the church and community. Some of these ministries include Youth, Love & Care, Social Justice, Saturday Prayer & Evangelism. Jesus saw the fruit of the church of Ephesus' labour, as well as the current churches of today. This is the reason He says in Mathew 5:16, "Let your light so shine before men, that they may see your good works, and glorify your Father which is in heaven." We must, First Timothy, continue to glorify our Father in heaven regardless of what is happening in our home, community, and world because Jesus knows our good works. In accordance with Revelation 2: 3, Jesus knows how First Timothy continues to persevere, thrive, grow, and overcome adverse situations such as a pandemic. Jesus moves in mysterious ways. His wonders to perform. As a testament, take a listen to this new gospel song titled "Good Works" by Kenneth Arnold, Jr. who was raised in the church at First Timothy and baptized by our pastor, Reverend Newbill.

## Key Point 2:

Secondly, Jesus condemned the church of Ephesus for abandoning the first love it had at first as recorded in Revelation 2: 4. According to the message from the Sunday Sermon, the church had love at the beginning but drifted spiritually from God. The church labored but it was not out of love for God and others. The church did not give, worship, serve, pray like it used to do. The church was opened but was just going through the moments. Apostle Paul explained it this way in 1 Corinthians 13:3, "And though I bestow all my goods to feed the poor, and though I give my body to be burned, and have not charity, it profiteth me nothing." In essence, "If I give away everything that I have and hand over my own body to feel good about what I have done but I don't have love, I receive no benefit whatsoever" (Common English Bible).

Thus, the church of Ephesus seemed to have everything but left thy first love. According to the Sunday Sermon message, the church loved its ministries, activities, itineraries, etc. but did not love Jesus more than these things. Do you love Jesus more than material things such as shopping, golfing, fishing, biking, bowling, and watching football? Jesus asked the Apostle Peter the same question in John 21:15. Peter, "Do you love me more than these things?" Peter replied, "Yes Lord, you know I love you."

Jesus loves us unconditionally. The little kids use to sing, "Jesus loves me this I know, for the bible tells me so." Jesus expects reciprocity from us as recorded in the gospel of Mark 12: 30 – 31: Verse 30 reads, "And thou shalt love the Lord thy God with all thy heart, and with all thy soul, and with all thy mind, and with all thy strength: this is the first commandment." Verse 31 reads, "And the second is namely this, Thou shalt love thy neighbour as thyself. There is no other commandment greater than these."

In brief, Jesus tells the church of Ephesus what it has done to offend Him which is the loss of its first love. According to the message from the Sunday Sermon, the church needs to be reminded of who is in control. For instance, the church thrives when everyone agrees that Christ is in control. When people are in control, our focus is on what pleases us. When Christ is in control, our focus is on what pleases him. When people are in control, we seek to have our way. When Christ is in control, we seek to yield to his way. When people are in control, we depend on our resources. When Christ is in control, we depend on God's resources. When people are in control, everyone seeks his own glory. When Christ is in control, everyone seeks God's glory. In essence, when Christ is in control, you will see ministries after ministries, miracles after miracles, and victories after victories. When Christ is in control, you will see love for everybody, joy in our home, community, and unity in the body of Christ. When Christ is in control, we know that we can overcome anything in life; so any church that has loss the first love has an obligation to ask the Lord to take me back as sang by Andre Crouch. The song reads, "Take me back, take me back dear Lord, where I first received you. Take me back, take me back dear Lord, where I first believed."

When Christ is in control, we know that we can overcome any tribulation. Jesus says in the gospel of John 16:33, "These things I have spoken unto you, that in me ye might have peace. In the world, ye shall have tribulation: but be of good cheer; I have overcome the world." Thus, Christ is a perfect father for us to overcome any tribulation. He is a father for us when we are fatherless. He is a mother for us when we are motherless. As an example, take a listen to a scene from the movie Overcome.

## Key Point 3:

Thirdly, Jesus calls for us to remember from which you have fallen, repent, and do the first works or I will come unto you quickly and remove your candlestick from its place if you don't repent (Revelation 2: 5). In other words, remember when you stopped coming to church faithfully, giving, witnessing, praising, and singing for the Lord.

With that said, Jesus calls for us to repent, return from our sins, respect ourselves, and follow him. Jesus corrects us because he loves us eternally. As a sign of love, a daddy must correct his or her child sometimes. He must distinguish the difference between daddy and child, so it is easy to correct him or her when needed. Do I have a witness? On the same note, Jesus must correct us also, but we must be receptive to his words. We must be receptive when he tells us to stop behaving, acting, and communicating in a way that is not in accordance with his commandments. Do I have a witness? Jesus wants us to have a house of worship where people say, "I was glad when they said unto me, let us go into the house of the Lord" (Psalm 122: 1) where people are being saved, praising the Lord, and providing ministries for the least, last, and lost. "For the Son of man is come to save that which is lost" (Matthew 18:11). Jesus is a problem solver. He has the solution to all our concerns. We must seek him for what we need. We must believe in what he commands and not the doctrine of some other religion (Revelation 2:6). We must love the house of worship a place where his glory resides (Psalms 26: 8).

I'm reminded of a Charlie Brown story. Can I tell the story? Okay. At the beginning of the week, Charlie Brown was looking miserable as usual. Lucy approached him and asked: "Discouraged again Charlie Brown?" Charlie Brown did not respond; so Lucy said, "You know what your trouble is?" Charlie Brown did not respond; so Lucy said, "The trouble with you is that you are you." Charlie Brown turned to her and said, well, "What in the world can I do about it?" Lucy replied, "I don't intend to give advice Charlie Brown; I basically point out the trouble." Aren't you glad that Jesus doesn't just point out the trouble? He provides us a solution when we are confronted with trouble. He provides us a solution when we are confronted with distress. He provides us a solution when we are confronted with unrest. Jesus says in the Gospel of 2 Chronicles 7: 14, "If my people, which are called by my name, shall humble themselves, and pray, and seek my face, and turn from their wicked ways; then will I hear from heaven, and will forgive their sin, and will heal their land." "Jesus says also in the Gospel of Romans 10: 9, "If thou shalt confess with thy mouth the Lord Jesus, and shalt believe in thine heart that God hath raised him from the dead, thou shalt be saved." As an example, take a listen to a scene from the movie Woodlawn.

In summary, this lesson focused on the words of commendation, condemnation, and correction. Jesus commends the church for its good works, condemns the church for abandoning the first love it had at first, and calls for the church to repent and do the first works or lose its candlestick. Amen.

At this time, let's reflect on some of the daily journal questions on "First Love" from the book, *"Beyond the Sunday Sermon."* Constance Holmes will lead the discussion.

We are now at the end of the bible study for 2023. We certainly hope you have gained something from this bible study. We have enjoyed facilitating the bible study for 12 weeks and could not have done this without your good works; and the vision of our pastor Reverend Newbill to relaunch the bible study at First Timothy in such a format. If we have any visitors in church tonight, please raise your hand so we can acknowledge your presence.

We thank you for your attendance in church and online. We wish you, First Timothy and friends, a joyful and wonderful Merry Christmas and Happy New Year!

We would like to leave you with a final song. Afterwards, we will have closing remarks from Minister Milton.

*Ronald W. Holmes, Ph.D.*

# WEEK 12: Outline of Service

Outline of Service<br>
First Timothy Wednesday Night Bible Study<br>
December 6, 2023<br>
7:00PM – 8:00PM

Message: Remember, Repent, Return & Respect!
from the book *"Beyond the Sunday Sermon"* (Pages 180 - 184)
Scripture: Revelation 2:1-7 KJV

| Time | What | By Whom | Music to play or Visual to Display |
|---|---|---|---|
| 6:53PM – 7:00PM | Song/video: I'll Just Say Yes by Brian Courtney Wilson (7:01) | Media Ministry to play song/video | • Play song/music – I'll Just Say Yes |
| 7:00PM -7:02PM | Prayer and Intro of Wednesday Night Bible Study | Minister Milton | • Show Slide 1 – Wednesday Night Bible Study |
| 7:02PM – 7:05PM | Intro & Teaching Method | Dr. Ronald Holmes | • Show Slide 2– Remember, Repent, Return, Respect<br>• Slide 3 – Rev. Frederick and Mrs. Newbill |
| 7:05PM – 7:10PM | Reading the Excerpt – Remember, Repent, Return, Respect | Constance Holmes | • Slide 4 – Remember, Repent, Return, Respect |
| 7:10PM – 7:15PM | • Three Key Points from the Message<br>• Point #1: Commendation/ 7 Churches of Revelation<br>• Whoever has ears | Dr. Ronald Holmes | • Slide 5 -Key Messages -<br>• Slide 6- Point 1: Commendation/ 7 Churches of Revelation<br>• Slide 7- Whoever has ears |
| 7:15PM –7:20PM | Song<br>• Good Works - Kenneth Arnold Jr. – 3:00 | Media Ministry to play music video | • Slide 8 - Kenneth Arnold Jr |

| 7:20PM –7:25PM | • Point #2 – Condemnation<br>• God is in Control | Dr. Ronald Holmes | • Slide 9 – Point# 2-Condemnation<br>• Slide 10 – God is in Control |
|---|---|---|---|
| 7:25PM – 7:28PM | Video:<br>• Overcomer –3:38 | Media Ministry to play music video | • Play Slide 11 until video starts<br>• Play Video – Overcomer |
| 7:28PM – 7:33PM | • Point #3 -Correction<br>• Charlie Brown Cartoon | Dr. Ronald Holmes | • Slide 12 – Point #3 – Correction<br>• Slide 13 – Charlie Brown Cartoon |
| 7:33PM –7:36PM | • Video: Woodlawn (3:01) | Media Ministry to play music video | • Slide 14 to show until video starts<br>• Play video - Woodlawn |
| 7:36PM – 7:37PM | • Summarize Three Key Points | Dr. Ronald Holmes | • Slide 15– Summary of Key Points |
| 7:37PM – 7:50PM | Facilitated discussion of Daily Journal from the Book-Pages 182- 184 | Constance Holmes | • Slides 16 - 18 - as each question is being discussed |
| 7:50PM – 7:52PM | • Bible Study 2023 | Dr. Ronald Holmes | • Slide 19 |
| 7:52PM – 7:55PM | • Video: Brian Courtney Wilson - Always Peace (3:28) | Media Ministry to play music video | • Slide 20 |
| 7:55PM – 8:00PM | Closing Comments & Prayer | Minister Milton | • Continue with Slide 21 |

- I'll Just Say Yes- https://www.youtube.com/watch?v=mZ_sMqDYWj8
- Good Works – See email that was sent to you.
- Overcomer - https://youtu.be/OkWzGTLgfTs
- Woodlawn - https://youtu.be/vGb4L1Mojl0?si=orUqyL15iEPK7MU8
- Always Peace- https://youtu.be/EXiwv0tWiAE?si=QaBpiOYW4qEm75J0
- Kenneth Arnold Jr. Music

# WEEK 12: Visual Slides

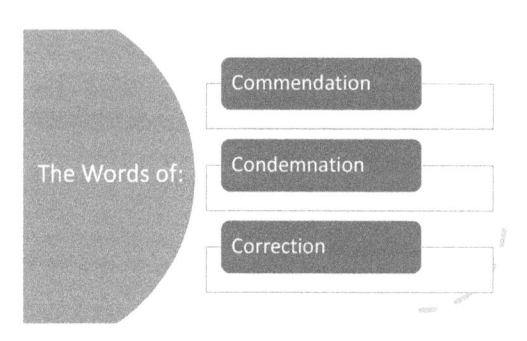

*A 12 Week Bible Study from the Devotional Book "Beyond the Sunday Sermon"*

1. Commendation

Kenneth
Arnold Jr.

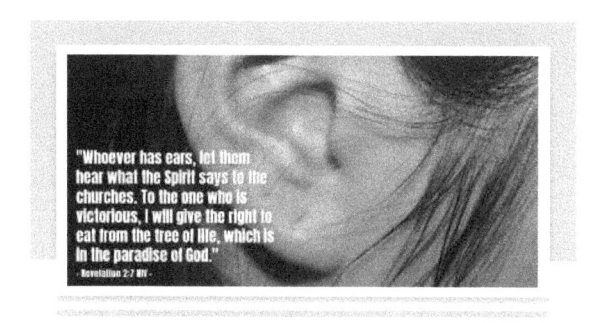

2. Condemnation

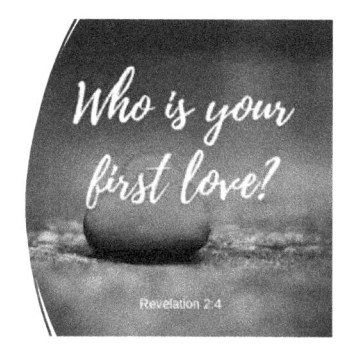

153

Ronald W. Holmes, Ph.D.

Overcomer!

3. Correction

Charlie Brown

154

*A 12 Week Bible Study from the Devotional Book "Beyond the Sunday Sermon"*

# WOODLAWN
THE TRUE STORY

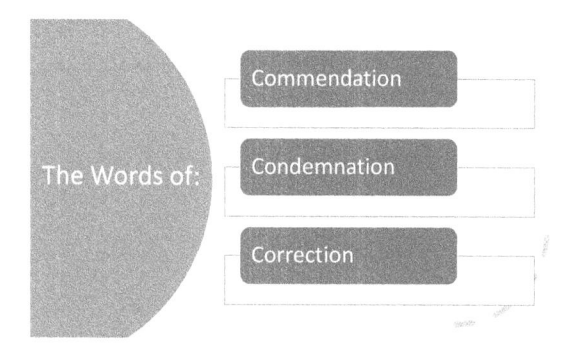

**The Words of:**
- Commendation
- Condemnation
- Correction

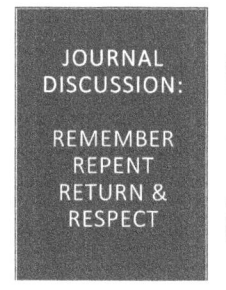

**JOURNAL DISCUSSION:**

REMEMBER
REPENT
RETURN &
RESPECT

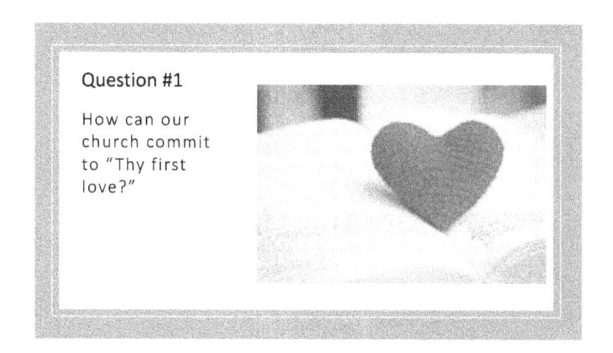

**Question #1**

How can our church commit to "Thy first love?"

Question #2
What is meant by the words, "do the first works" and "candlestick?"

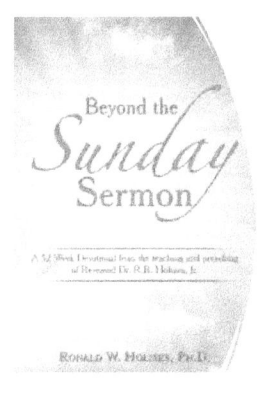

# Bible Study 2023

## 12 Weeks!
## Thank You!!!

One Last Song to hold us.....

Brian Courtney Wilson
Always Peace

## Closing REMARKS

# REFERENCES

Bowlby, K. (2022). 20 Powerful Martin Luther King Jr. quotes to remind you of his message. https://www.countryliving.com/life/inspirational-stories/g38736601/mlkquotes/?utm source=google&utm medium=cpc&utm

Common English Bible.

Goodreads.com. Martin Luther King Jr. quotes. Retrieved from https://goodreads.com/quotes/757-everybody-can-be-greatbecause-anybody-can-serve-you-don-t-have

Holmes, R.B. & Evans, A.L. (2016). Dr. R.B. Holmes…A visionary leader: memoirs, ministries, and messages. Blomington, IN: AuthorHouse.

Holmes, R.W. (2023). Beyond the Sunday Sermon. A 52 Devotional from the teaching and preaching of Reverend Dr. R.B. Holmes, Jr. Blomington, IN: Authorhouse.

Holmes, R.W. (2014). How to revitalize the National Baptist Convention, USA, Inc. Blomington, IN: Authorhouse.

King James Version. Holy Bible.

# AUTHOR'S BACKGROUND

Dr. Ronald Holmes is the author of 27 books and publisher of The Holmes Education Post, an education focused Internet newspaper. Holmes is a former teacher, school administrator, test developer and district superintendent. He has written children's books about the coronavirus, solar system, flowers, careers, and school bullying. His adult books focus on religion, hazing, workplace bullying, bipolar disorders, issues in education and completing the dissertation. Holmes earned a Ph.D. in Educational Leadership, a ME.D. in Educational Administration and Supervision and a B.S. in Business Education from Florida A&M University. He also earned a ME.D. in Business Education from Bowling Green State University. He has proven success working with students from the elementary to the collegiate level.

# OTHER BOOKS OF THE HOLMES EDUCATION POST, LLC

How to Revitalize the National Baptist Convention, USA, Inc.

Beyond the Sunday Sermon

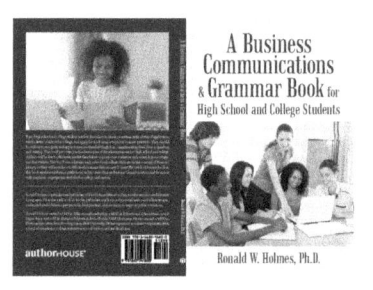

A Business Communications & Grammar Book for High School & College Students

Your Answers to Bipolar Disorder

Completing the Dissertation

Professional Career Paths

How to Eradicate Hazing

Jacob's Dream! A Story of Animals in Africa

How to Eradicate Workplace Bullying

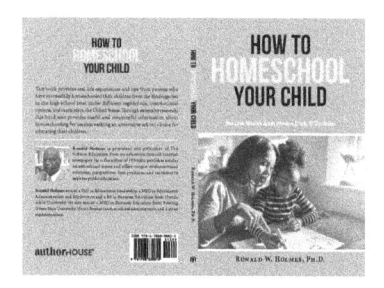

How to Homeschool Your Child

Current Issues & Answers in Education

Eradicating Cyber Bullying

Milton Keynes UK
Ingram Content Group UK Ltd.
UKHW040640140324
439347UK00012BB/157/J